A-Level Year 1 & AS
Psychology
Exam Board: AQA

Revising for Psychology exams is stressful, that's for sure — even just getting your
notes sorted out can leave you needing a lie down. But help is at hand...

This brilliant CGP book explains **everything you'll need to learn** (and nothing you won't),
with plenty of **in-depth psychological studies** to back up the theory. And of course,
it's all written in a straightforward style that's easy to get your head around.

We've also included **exam-style questions** for every topic, along with a section
of advice on how to pick up as many marks as possible in the final tests!

A-Level revision? It has to be CGP!

Published by CGP

Editors:
Katherine Faudemer, Ceara Hayden, Kirstie McHale, Camilla Simson

Contributors:
Richard Carciofo, Tracey Jones, Christine Johnson, Denise Say

ISBN: 978 1 78294 329 7

With thanks to Lauren Burns, Angela Jones and Glenn Rogers for the proofreading.
With thanks to Jan Greenway for the copyright research.

Cover image © Andrey Prokhorov/iStockphoto.com.

Clipart from Corel®
Printed by Elanders Ltd, Newcastle upon Tyne.

Based on the classic CGP style created by Richard Parsons.

Contents

We deliberately haven't put any answers in this book, because they'd just be saying what's already in the book. So instead, here's how to write answers and do well.

Conformity

Social psychology looks at how people interact and influence each other. Social influence means people change their behaviour to fit the situation or who they're with — for example, you might act differently with a parent than with a friend.

There's **More Than One Type** of **Conformity**

The influence of others can cause individuals to change their behaviour — this is **social influence**.
Conformity is when the behaviour of an individual or small group is **influenced** by a larger or dominant group.
There are **three** different types of conformity:

Internalisation means accepting the majority's views as your own

1) **Internalisation** is going along with the majority and **believing** in their views —
   you've accepted and **internalised** them so they're now your own too.
2) This might happen if you're in an unfamiliar situation, where you don't know what
   the 'correct' way to behave is. In this situation, you'd look to others for **information**
   about how to behave. This type of influence is called **informational social influence**.

Compliance is going along with things even if you disagree with them

1) **Compliance** is where you go along with the majority, even if you don't share their views.
2) You do this just to appear '**normal**' — going against the majority might lead to exclusion
   or rejection from the group. This type of influence is called **normative social influence**.

Identification means doing what's expected of you to fulfil a role

1) **Identification** is conforming to what's expected of you to fulfil a **social role**.
2) This means changing your behaviour because you want to fit a specific **role in society** (e.g. a nurse),
   or trying to imitate the behaviour of a **role model**. There's more about social roles on pages 5-6.

Sherif (1935) Tested the Effects of **Informational Social Influence**

Sherif researched whether people are influenced by others when they're doing an **ambiguous task**
(one where the answer isn't clear).

Sherif (1935) — Conformity and the autokinetic effect

Method:	This was a **laboratory experiment** with a **repeated measures** design. Sherif used a visual illusion called the **autokinetic effect**, where a stationary spot of light, viewed in a dark room, appears to move. Participants were falsely told that the experimenter would move the light. They had to estimate how far it had moved. In the first phase, individual participants made repeated estimates. They were then put into groups of 3 people, where they each made their estimate with the others present. Finally, they were retested individually.
Results:	When they were alone, participants developed their own stable estimates **(personal norms)**, which varied widely between participants. Once the participants were in a group, the estimates tended to **converge** and become more alike. When the participants were then retested on their own, their estimates were more like the **group estimates** than their original guesses.
Conclusion:	Participants were influenced by the estimates of other people, and a **group norm** developed. Estimates converged because participants used information from others to help them — they were affected by **informational social influence**.
Evaluation:	This was a **laboratory experiment**, so there was strict control of the variables. This means that the results are unlikely to have been affected by a third variable, so it should be possible to establish **cause and effect**. It also means that the method could be **replicated**. The **repeated measures** design meant that **participant variables** that could have affected the results were kept constant. However, the method is flawed because the participants were being asked to judge the movement of a light that wasn't moving — this rarely happens in real life. Because it created an **artificial situation**, the study can be criticised for lacking **ecological validity**. As well as this, the **sample** used was quite limited — all of the participants were male, so the results can't be **generalised** to everyone. An **ethical problem** with this study was **deception** — the participants were told the light was moving when it wasn't.

Conformity

Asch (1951) *Looked at the Effects of* **Normative Social Influence**

Asch designed an experiment to see whether people would conform to a majority's incorrect answer in an **unambiguous task** (one where the answer is obvious).

Asch (1951) — Conformity on an unambiguous task

Method: Asch carried out a **laboratory experiment** with an **independent groups** design. In groups of 8, participants judged line lengths (shown below) by saying out loud which comparison line (1, 2 or 3) matched the standard line. Each group contained only one real participant — the others were confederates (who acted like real participants but were really helping the experimenter). The real participant always went last or last but one, so that they heard the others' answers before giving theirs. Each participant did 18 trials. On 12 of these (the **critical trials**) the confederates all gave the same wrong answer. There was also a **control group**, where the participants judged the line lengths in isolation.

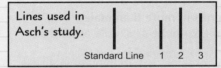

Lines used in Asch's study.
Standard Line   1   2   3

Seating plan for Asch's study.
The real participant was always in position 7 or 8 and the others were confederates.
① ② ③ ④ ⑤ ⑥ ⑦ ⑧
Stimulus Display

Results: In the control trials, participants gave the wrong answer **0.7%** of the time. In the critical trials, participants **conformed** to the majority (gave the same wrong answer) **37%** of the time. **75%** conformed at least once. Afterwards, some participants said they didn't really believe their answers, but didn't want to look different.

Conclusion: The control condition showed that the task was easy to get right. However, 37% were wrong on the critical trials — they conformed to the majority due to **normative social influence**.

Evaluation: This was a **laboratory experiment**, so there was **good control** of the variables. This minimises the effects of **extraneous variables**. Strict control of the variables also means that you could easily **repeat** the study to see if you get the same results. However, because the participants weren't in a **natural situation**, the study lacks **ecological validity**. Whether they were right or wrong didn't really matter to the participants — they might have been less likely to conform if their answer had had real-life consequences. In terms of **ethics**, the participants were **deceived** and might have been embarrassed when they found out the true nature of the study.

Asch's *Participants were Influenced by* **Situational Factors**

Sometimes we're influenced by others and conform, but sometimes we resist these influences and behave **independently**. There are **situational** and **dispositional** factors that affect conformity. Situational factors are due to the **social situation** a person is in, whereas dispositional factors are due to the person's **internal characteristics**. Asch investigated **situational factors**:

1)   Group Size

You might expect that the bigger the majority is, the more influential it will be. If that was the case, it would be easier to resist conforming when there were fewer people to influence you. To test this, Asch (1956) conducted his conformity experiment with different numbers of confederates as the majority.

With only two confederates, the real participant conformed on only 14% of the critical trials. With three confederates, conformity rose to 32%. There was little change to conformity rates after that — no matter how big the majority group got. So, very small majorities are easier to resist than larger ones. But influence doesn't keep increasing with the size of the majority.

2)   Unanimity / Social Support

Asch absolutely loved doing his conformity experiment, so he ran yet another version of it to test the effect of having a **supporter** in the group. Rather than the confederates forming a **unanimous majority**, one of the confederates **agreed** with the **participant**.

Having a fellow **dissenter** (someone who disagrees with the majority) broke the **unanimity** of the group, which made it easier for the participant to **resist** the pressure to conform — the rate of conformity **fell** to **5.5%**.

3)   Task Difficulty

When Asch made the task **more difficult** by making the lines more similar, conformity levels increased.

People are more likely to conform if they're less **confident** that they're correct — there's more about this on the next page.

Conformity

Dispositional factors also affect conformity...

Confidence and Expertise Might Affect Conformity

When Asch **debriefed** his participants, he found a common factor of **confidence** in the people who hadn't conformed. If someone felt confident in their judgements, they were more able to **resist** group pressure.

1) **Wiesenthal et al (1976)** found that if people felt **competent** in a task, they were **less likely** to conform.

2) **Perrin and Spencer (1980)** replicated Asch's study with participants who were engineering students. Conformity levels were much **lower**. This could have been due to the fact that engineers had **confidence** in their skills in making accurate observations.

Gender Might Also be a Factor

Until the mid-1970s, the dominant view was that **females conform more than males**. Then **Eagly and Carli** did a load of research that suggests it might not be as simple as all that...

Eagly and Carli (1981) did a **meta-analysis** of conformity research, where they re-analysed data from a number of studies. They did find some sex differences in conformity, but the differences were **inconsistent**. The clearest difference between men and women was in **Asch**-like studies where there was **group pressure** from an **audience**.

Eagly (1987) argued that men and women's **different social roles** explain the difference in conformity — women are more concerned with **group harmony**, so are more likely to agree with others. **Assertiveness** and **independence** are valued male attributes, so maintaining your own opinion under pressure fits with the perceived male social role.

Practice Questions

Q1 What is normative social influence?

Q2 What type of social influence did Sherif's study investigate?

Q3 Outline the strengths and weaknesses of the research method in Asch's study.

Q4 What situational factors did Asch identify that affected conformity levels?

Exam Questions

Q1 Which of the terms A, B, C, D or E best matches the statement below?

> Looking to others for guidance because you lack knowledge of how to behave.

A conformity
B informational social influence
C internalisation
D normative social influence
E compliance

[1 mark]

Q2 Explain what is meant by identification.

[3 marks]

Q3 Describe and evaluate **two** studies of conformity.

[12 marks]

Q4 Discuss **two** variables that affect conformity.

[6 marks]

Oh doobee doo, I wanna be like you-oo-oo...

Social influence just means changing your behaviour because of what other people are doing or saying. Conformity is also known as majority influence — it means changing your behaviour to fit in with the rest of the group (the majority). Conformity might not happen in all situations, and some people are more likely to conform than others. Asch showed this in different versions of his study — make sure you know what effect these different set-ups had on conformity.

Conformity to Social Roles

People adopt different behaviours depending on the role they want to play in society. Where it gets interesting is that people conform to roles by adopting the behaviour associated with them, even if the roles are randomly assigned...

Social Roles are the Behaviours that Society Expects from You

1) People hold different **positions** in society, such as teenager, grandparent, manager, priest, etc. Most people occupy several positions at the same time — e.g. student, waiter, brother and son.

2) **Social roles** are the sets of **behaviours** and **expectations** that come with holding these positions.

3) For example, in our society a woman who has a baby might be expected to look after and love her child — these are the behaviours that fulfil the social role of '**mother**'.

4) The expectations of a role are held by society. When we accept a role, we **internalise** these expectations so that they shape our behaviour.

Zimbardo et al (1973) Studied Conformity to Social Roles

Zimbardo et al set up a mock prison to see if people would conform to the **assigned roles** of prisoner or guard.

Zimbardo et al (1973) — Stanford prison experiment

Method:	Male students were recruited to act as either guards or prisoners in a mock prison. They were randomly given the roles of prisoner or guard, and their behaviour was observed. The prisoners were 'arrested' as they went about their day, taken to 'prison' and given uniforms and numbers. The guards also wore uniforms and mirrored sunglasses.
Results:	Initially, the guards tried to assert their authority and the prisoners resisted by sticking together. The prisoners then became more passive and obedient, while the guards invented nastier punishments. The experiment was abandoned early because some prisoners became very distressed.
Conclusion:	Guards and prisoners adopted their social roles quickly. Zimbardo claims this shows that our **social role can influence our behaviour** — seemingly well-balanced men became unpleasant and aggressive in the role of guard.
Evaluation:	This was a **controlled observation**, so there was **good control** of variables. However, because it was an artificial environment, the results can't really be **generalised** to real-life situations. In terms of **ethics**, some participants found the experience very distressing. There's also a problem with **observer bias**, as Zimbardo ran the prison himself, and later admitted that he became too personally involved in the situation. The conclusion Zimbardo reached doesn't explain why only some of the participants acted according to their assigned roles.

Studies can help Explain how Social Roles Affect People in the Real World

1) No one has ever replicated Zimbardo's prison study exactly. This has been down to design problems, such as making it an **ethical** experiment.

2) However, there have been other similar studies into **assigned roles**. One of these was done by **Orlando (1973)**.

Psychologists have to design their experiments to meet ethical guidelines, otherwise they can't be carried out — see pages 91-92 for the guidelines produced by the British Psychological Society.

Orlando (1973) set up a **mock psychiatric ward** in a hospital for three days. 29 staff members of the hospital volunteered to be 'patients', and were held in the ward. Another 22 staff members were involved, but they were just asked to carry out their normal daily roles.

It only took a little while for the 'patients' to start **behaving** like real patients of the hospital. It became very difficult to tell them apart — they seemed to be **conforming** to the roles that had been assigned to them. Many showed signs of depression and withdrawal, and six even tried to escape from the ward.

After the study, the mock patients reported that they had felt frustrated, anxious and despairing. Some felt that they'd **lost their identity**, that their feelings weren't important, and that they weren't being treated as people.

3) Studies like this can give really useful information about how **real patients** might feel in a hospital. Orlando's (1973) study led to more of an effort by the staff to respect the patients, and improved the relationship and cooperation between them.

Conformity to Social Roles

Zimbardo's study has never been exactly replicated, but similar studies have tried to find out more about conformity...

Reicher and Haslam (2006) Developed the Ideas in Zimbardo's Study

1) In the **Holocaust** during World War Two, approximately 6 million Jews were horrifically murdered by the Nazis.
2) Psychologists had different theories about the soldiers who'd carried out the killings. Some thought they must be 'evil', but others thought they were 'normal' people who'd committed atrocities because of their **social role**.
3) **Zimbardo's** (1973) study showed that normal people will shape their behaviour to fit into a social role, even if it's only been randomly assigned.
4) It seemed that the participants' behaviour was **situational**, rather than **dispositional**.
5) **Reicher and Haslam** (2006) recreated a similar situation to Zimbardo's experiment, but they were particularly interested to see how the group dynamics changed over time.

Reicher and Haslam (2006) — The BBC prison study

Method:	This was a **controlled observation** in a mock prison, which was filmed for television. The participants were 15 male volunteers who had responded to an advert. They were randomly assigned to 2 groups — 5 were guards and 10 were prisoners. They had daily tests to measure levels of depression, compliance with rules, and stress. The prisoners knew that one of them, chosen **at random**, would become a guard after 3 days. An independent **ethics committee** had the power to stop the experiment at any time in order to protect the participants.
Results:	The guards failed to form a united group and identify with their role. They didn't always exercise their power and said they felt uncomfortable with the inequality of the situation. In the first 3 days, the prisoners tried to act in a way that would get them promoted to guard status. After one was promoted, they became a much **stronger group** because they knew there were no more chances of promotion. The unequal system collapsed due to the **unwillingness of the guards** and the **strength of the prisoner group**. On Day 6 the prisoners rebelled and the participants decided to live in a democracy, but this also collapsed due to tensions within the group. Some of the former prisoners then wanted to set up a stricter regime with them as leaders. The study was **abandoned** early on the advice of the ethics committee, as the participants showed signs of stress.
Conclusion:	The participants didn't fit into their expected social roles, suggesting that these roles are **flexible**.
Evaluation:	In contrast to Zimbardo's findings, Reicher and Haslam's prisoners were a strong group, and the guards were weak. However, it's possible that this was because Reicher and Haslam's guards were not as empowered as Zimbardo's, who were actively encouraged to maintain order. This study has been criticised for being made for TV — many people (including Zimbardo) argued that elements of it were staged and the participants played up to the cameras. Because this was an artificial situation, the results can't be **generalised** to real life. The **ethics** of this study were good — the participants were not **deceived**, so they were able to give **informed consent**. The participants were **protected** by the ethics committee and the study was abandoned as soon as they appeared to be becoming stressed. They were also **debriefed** and offered counselling afterwards.

Practice Questions

Q1 What is a social role?
Q2 What's the difference between situational and dispositional behaviour?

Exam Questions

Q1	Briefly outline and evaluate identification with social roles as an explanation for conformity.	[4 marks]
Q2	Describe and evaluate the findings of one study on conformity to social roles.	[8 marks]

Who knew role-play was so popular?

Conformity's handy because it means you don't have to make any decisions for yourself... It's all about wanting to fit in with a group, even if you think it's actually a bit rubbish. Personally I reckon joining a group that involves being arrested and put in a fake prison isn't really ideal. I'd probably just say thanks but I'm washing my hair that week.

Obedience to Authority

Atteeennnnnnnnnnnnshun! Obedience means acting in response to a direct order, usually from an authority figure.

Milgram (1963) Studied Obedience

Milgram (1963) — Obedience to Authority

Method:	Milgram conducted a number of **laboratory experiments** to test factors thought to affect obedience. This condition tested whether people would obey orders to shock someone in a separate room. It took place at the prestigious Yale University. **40 men** participated, responding to newspaper adverts seeking **volunteers** for a study on 'learning and memory'. They received payment for attending, which didn't depend on them proceeding with the experiment. The experimenter wore a grey technician's coat. Each participant was introduced to a **confederate** (acting like a participant, but who was really part of the experimental set-up). They drew lots to see who would act as 'teacher' and 'learner', but this was fixed so the participant was always the teacher. The participant witnessed the confederate being strapped into a chair and connected up to a shock generator in the next room. It didn't actually give electric shocks, but the participants thought it was real. The switches ranged from 15 volts (labelled 'Slight Shock') to 450 volts (labelled 'XXX'). The participant taught the learner word-pairs over an intercom. When the learner answered incorrectly, the participant had to administer an **increasing level of shock**. After the 300 V shock, the learner pounded on the wall and made no further responses. If participants hesitated during the process, the experimenter told them to continue. **Debriefing** included an interview, questionnaires and being reunited with the 'learner'.
Results:	**26 participants (65%)** administered **450 V** and **none stopped before administering 300 V** (when the learner banged on the wall). Most participants showed obvious signs of stress like sweating, groaning and trembling.
Conclusion:	**Ordinary people** will **obey orders** to hurt someone else, even if it means acting against their conscience.

Milgram's Experiment had Good and Bad Points

1) **Internal validity**: It's possible that participants didn't really believe they were inflicting electric shocks — they were just going along with the **experimenter's expectations** (showing **demand characteristics**). But Milgram claimed participants' **stressed reactions** showed they believed the experiment was real.

2) **Ecological validity**: Milgram's participants did a task that they were unlikely to encounter in real life (shocking someone). So the study **lacks ecological validity**. However, because it was a **laboratory experiment** there was good control of the variables, so it's possible to establish **cause and effect**.

3) **Ethical issues**: The participants were **deceived** as to the true nature of the study. This means they couldn't give **informed consent**. They weren't informed of their **right to withdraw** from the experiment. In fact, they were prompted to continue when they wanted to stop. The participants showed signs of stress during the experiment, so they weren't **protected**. However, they were extensively **debriefed** and 84% of them said they were pleased to have taken part. As well as this, at the time of the experiment there weren't any formal ethical guidelines in place, so technically Milgram didn't breach any. There's more general stuff on ethics on pages 91-93.

Milgram Identified Situational Factors that Affected Obedience

Milgram carried out his experiment in loads of slightly different ways to investigate the effect that certain conditions would have on the results.

1) **Presence of allies** — When there were 3 teachers (1 participant and 2 confederates), the real participant was **less likely to obey** if the other two refused to obey. Having **allies** can make it easier to resist orders.

2) **Proximity of the victim** — Milgram's results suggest an important factor was the **proximity (closeness)** of the **learner**. In the condition described above, 65% gave the maximum shock. This dropped to 40% with the learner in the **same room**, and 30% when the participant had to put the learner's hand onto the shock plate. Proximity made the learner's suffering harder to ignore.

3) **Proximity of the authority** — When the authority figure gave prompts by **phone** from another room, obedience rates dropped to 23%. When the authority figure wasn't close by, orders were **easier to resist**.

4) **Location of the experiment** — When the participants were told the study was being run by a private company, and the experiment was moved to a set of **run-down offices** in a nearby town, the proportion of people giving the maximum shock fell to 48%. When his association with a prestigious university (Yale) was removed, the authority of the experimenter seemed **less legitimate**, so the participants were more likely to question it. (There's more about legitimate authority on the next page.)

Obedience to Authority

There are lots of explanations for why people obey authority...

Milgram's **Agency Theory (1973)** Explains **Obedience**

1) When people behave on behalf of an **external authority** (do as they're told), they're said to be in an **agentic state**. This means they act as someone's **agent**, rather than taking personal responsibility for their actions.

2) The opposite of this is behaving **autonomously** — not following orders.

3) Milgram's **agency theory** stated that when we feel we're acting out the wishes of another person (being their agent), we feel **less responsible** for our actions.

4) This effect is seen in Milgram's studies. Some participants were concerned for the **welfare** of the learner and asked who would take **responsibility** if the learner was harmed. When the experimenter (authority) took responsibility, often the participant would continue.

5) This **agentic state** was also encouraged by the experiment's set-up. The participants voluntarily entered a **social contract** (an obligation) with the experimenter to take part and follow the procedure of the study.

6) People can start off acting in an **autonomous** way (thinking for themselves), but then become obedient. This is known as an **agentic shift**. When Milgram's participants arrived for the experiment they were in an **autonomous state**, but as soon as they started following orders they underwent an **agentic shift**, and entered an **agentic state**.

7) Milgram claimed that there were some **binding factors** that might have kept his participants in the **agentic state**:

> • **Reluctance** to **disrupt the experiment** — participants had already been paid, so may have felt **obliged** to continue.
>
> • The **pressure** of the **surroundings** — the experiment took place in a prestigious university (see previous page). This made the experimenter seem like a **legitimate authority** (see below).
>
> • The **insistence** of the **authority figure** — if participants hesitated they were told that they **had** to continue the experiment.

Milgram's **Agency Theory** is **Supported** by his **Results**

Before his studies, Milgram believed that people were **autonomous** and could **choose** to resist authority. His **agency theory** shows Milgram's findings changed his mind about how much impact authority figures have.

Evaluation of Agency Theory

1) There's lots of **experimental evidence** to support agency theory — Milgram's participants often claimed they wouldn't have gone as far by themselves, but they were just following orders.

2) Sometimes people **resist** the pressure to obey authority. This can be because of the situation, or because of individual differences (see page 10). Agency theory doesn't explain why some people are more likely to exhibit **independent behaviour** (i.e. resist pressure to conform or obey) than others.

Obedience Can Depend on the **Legitimacy** of the **Authority**

1) We're socialised to recognise the authority of people like **parents, police officers, doctors, teachers**, etc.

2) These kinds of people are **legitimate authorities** — they're given the **right** to **tell us what to do**. This means we're more likely to obey them.

3) Legitimate authority comes from having a **defined social role** which people **respect** — usually because it implies **knowledge** or comes with **legal power**.

4) When Milgram re-ran his study in some **run-down offices**, obedience rates were lower than when the study was run in the university (see previous page).

5) He argued that the experimenter's authority was higher in the university situation because of the **status** of the university.

6) **Bickman (1974)** conducted a field experiment where researchers ordered passers-by to do something like pick up a bit of litter. They were dressed either in a guard's uniform, as a milkman, or just in smart clothes. People were much more likely to obey the person in a guard's uniform. This was because he seemed to be the most **legitimate authority figure**.

Obedience to Authority

The **Authoritarian Personality** Can Also Explain **Obedience**

1) Adorno's theory of the **authoritarian personality** is a **dispositional** (personality) explanation of obedience.

2) **Adorno et al (1950)** proposed that **over-strict parenting** results in a child being socialised to **obey authority unquestioningly**, because they learn strict obedience to their parents.

3) Adorno expanded on this idea to argue that strict parenting also resulted in **prejudice**:
   - Strict parenting means the child feels **constrained**, which creates **aggression**.
   - But the child is afraid they'll be **disciplined** if they express this aggression towards their parents, so instead they're hostile to people they see as weak or **inferior** to them — usually minority groups.

4) Adorno et al defined the collection of traits that they thought resulted from over-strict parenting as the **authoritarian personality**. As well as **aggression** to people of perceived **lower status**, and **blind obedience**, the identifying traits included being **conformist** and having **rigid moral standards**.

The F-scale	Adorno et al (1950) developed a scale to measure how strongly people express **authoritarian traits**, called the **F-scale**. *The 'F' stands for fascism.*

This research began shortly after the end of the Second World War — Adorno's team were trying to find out if there are characteristics of individuals which could explain the persecution of Jews and other minority groups by the Nazis in the 1930s and 40s.

Evaluation of Adorno's Authoritarian Personality Theory

1) **Elms and Milgram (1966)** found that participants who scored higher on the **F-scale** (so had more authoritarian traits) had been willing to administer bigger shocks in Milgram's experiment.

2) However, this doesn't necessarily mean that a strict upbringing or having authoritarian traits **causes** people to be obedient — other factors such as **education** could cause both authoritarian traits and obedience.

3) Also, Milgram found that **situational factors** like proximity and location (see page 7) had a bigger effect on obedience.

4) The theory also doesn't explain how **whole societies** can become obedient — not everybody has this personality type.

Practice Questions

Q1 Outline the method of Milgram's (1963) experiment.
Q2 In Milgram's 1963 experiment, what percentage of participants gave the maximum shock?
Q3 Why was the validity of Milgram's study criticised?
Q4 What is meant by 'proximity' and why is it a factor in obedience?
Q5 What is meant by an 'agentic shift'?
Q6 Why might obedience rates have dropped when Milgram's study took place in run-down offices?
Q7 What does the F-scale measure?

Exam Questions

Q1 Evaluate Milgram's (1963) study of obedience in terms of ethical issues.	[6 marks]
Q2 Outline **two** situational variables that may affect obedience.	[4 marks]
Q3 Outline and evaluate the agentic state as an explanation for obedience.	[4 marks]
Q4 Describe and evaluate the authoritarian personality as an explanation for obedience.	[6 marks]

Pretty shocking results, don't you think?

Milgram crops up all the time, so you need to learn this stuff well. You've got to admit it's pretty incredible that people would give someone a 450 V shock just because they were told to. Everyone thinks that they wouldn't have done it if they were one of the participants, but really it's impossible to know. I definitely would have though. I love electricity.

Resistance to Social Influence

So why, you might ask, do some people resist social influence where others don't? It's an intriguing question...

Having **Social Support** Can Make People **More** Resistant

1) More of Milgram's participants resisted orders if there were **other participants present** who refused to obey (see page 7). This suggests that people find it easier to stand up to authority if they have support from others, because they no longer have to take full responsibility for rebelling.

2) This ties in with Asch's research on conformity. He found that participants were more likely to resist the pressure to conform if one of the confederates **agreed** with them (page 3). It seems that people are more likely to display independent behaviour if they've got **support** from others.

3) It doesn't really make sense to call this behaviour **independent**, seeing as it depends on having someone else there to agree with you... But just go with it...

Aspects of **Personality** May Influence **Independent Behaviour**

Your resistance to social influence might also be affected by a personality characteristic called **locus of control**. This indicates how much **personal control** you believe you have over events in your life.

The idea is that people who feel they're generally in control of what happens in their life are more likely to resist — this is a **dispositional explanation** for resistance.

1) **Rotter (1966)** developed a **questionnaire** to **measure locus of control**.

2) The questionnaire involved choosing between **paired statements** like these ones:

> A: Misfortune is usually brought about by people's own actions.
>
> B: Things that make us unhappy are largely due to bad luck.

If you agree with the first statement, you have an **internal locus of control**. This is categorised by a belief that what happens in your life results from **your own behaviour or actions**.
E.g. if you did well in a test you might put it down to how much work you did for it.

If you agree with the second statement, you have an **external locus of control**. This is a belief that events are caused by external factors, like **luck** or the **actions of others**.
E.g. if you did well in a test you might put it down to good questions coming up, or a lenient examiner.

3) People with an **internal locus of control** feel a stronger sense of control over their lives than people with an **external locus of control**. This means that they're more likely to exhibit **independent behaviour** — i.e. they're less likely to conform or obey.

4) People with an **external locus of control** may be more likely to conform or obey.

Practice Questions

Q1 What's the difference between an internal and an external locus of control?

Exam Questions

Q1 Which **two** of the following are factors which may make resistance to social influence more likely?

A the agentic state **B** an internal locus of control **C** unanimity of the group
D social support **E** an external locus of control [2 marks]

Q2 Explain how an individual's personality can make them more likely to resist social influence. [4 marks]

Resisting social pressure to stop making terrible jokes is really hard. Seriously.

Some things make resisting social influence easier — social support and having an internal locus of control are the key ones. A lot of it's common sense really — people are more likely to do what everybody else is doing if they're the only one that's different, but if you see yourself as in control or you feel responsible then you might be able to resist.

Minority Influence and Social Change

So far most of this social influence stuff has been about majority influence, but that's not the only type of social influence. Minorities can have social influence too — funnily enough this is called minority influence.

Minority Influence *Can be Quite* **Powerful**

1) Obviously people don't always go along with the majority — if they did, nothing would ever change.
2) Sometimes **small minorities** and even **individuals** gain influence and change the way the majority thinks.
3) In **minority influence**, it seems that a form of **internalisation** (see page 2) is taking place. Members of the majority actually take on the beliefs and views of a **consistent minority** — rather than just complying.

Minority Influence *is* **Stronger** *if the Minority...*

... is **Consistent**

Moscovici et al (1969) did some research into **minority influence** that compared **inconsistent** minorities with **consistent** minorities.

Moscovici et al (1969) — Minority influence

Method:	This was a laboratory experiment into **minority influence** using 192 women. In groups of 6 at a time, participants judged the colour of 36 slides. All of the slides were blue, but the brightness of the blue varied. Two of the six participants in each group were **confederates**. In one condition the confederates called all 36 slides 'green' (consistent) and in another condition they called 24 of the slides 'green' and 12 of the slides 'blue' (inconsistent). A control group was also used which contained no confederates.
Results:	In the **control group** the participants called the slides 'green' **0.25%** of the time. In the **consistent** condition **8.4%** of the time participants adopted the minority position and called the slides 'green', and **32%** of the participants called the slides 'green' at least once. In the **inconsistent** condition the participants moved to the minority position of calling the slides 'green' only **1.25%** of the time.
Conclusion:	The confederates were in the **minority** but their views appear to have influenced the real participants. The use of the two conditions illustrated that the minority **had more influence** when they were **consistent** in calling the slides 'green'.
Evaluation:	This study was a laboratory experiment, so it **lacked ecological validity** because the task was artificial. The participants may have felt that judging the colour of the slide was a **trivial** exercise — they might have acted differently if their principles were involved. Also, the study was only carried out on women, so the results can't be generalised to men. However, owing to the use of a **control** group, we know that the participants were actually influenced by the minority rather than being independently unsure of the colour of the slides. In a similar experiment, participants were asked to **write down** the colour rather than saying it out loud. In this condition, even more people agreed with the minority, which provides **more support** for minority influence.

... is **Flexible**

Nemeth et al (1974) repeated Moscovici's experiment, but instructed participants to answer with **all of the colours** they saw in the slide, rather than a single colour. For example, they could answer 'green-blue' rather than 'green'.

They ran **three variations** — where the two confederates:

1) said **all** of the slides were 'green'
2) said the slides were 'green' or 'green-blue' at **random**
3) said the **brighter** slides were 'green-blue' and the **duller** slides were 'green' or vice versa

When the confederates always answered 'green', or varied their response randomly (so were **inconsistent**), they had no effect on the participants' responses. But in the condition where the confederates responses **varied** with a feature of the slides (the brightness), the confederates had a **significant effect** on the participants' responses.

The confederates had most influence when they were **consistent but flexible** — Nemeth proposed that rigid consistency (always answering 'green') wasn't effective because it seemed **unrealistic** when more subtle responses were allowed.

Minority Influence and Social Change

There are different theories about how minority influence works — some people think it can be explained by the same process as majority influence, but some people think it's a completely different kettle of fish...

Moscovici's **Conversion Theory** Says **Minority Influence** Works **Differently**

Moscovici's **conversion theory** (1980) suggests that majority and minority influence are **different processes**:

Majority Influence

People **compare their behaviour** to the majority (social comparison), and change their behaviour to **fit in** without considering the majority's views in detail.

So majority influence involves **compliance** — it doesn't always cause people to change their private feelings, just their behaviour.

Minority Influence

When a minority is consistent people may actually **examine** the minority's beliefs in detail because they want to **understand why** the minority sees things differently.

This can lead to people **privately accepting** the minority view — they **convert** to the minority position.

Social pressure to **conform** may mean their behaviour doesn't actually change, at least at first.

Minorities Can **Change Views** When They're **Committed**

In his conversion theory Moscovici described the **factors** that he thought enabled minority influence to happen — the main factor was **consistency**, which shows **commitment**:

1) Initially, minority views can be seen as **wrong**, because they don't match up with what's considered the **norm**.

2) But by being **consistent** the minority group shows that it has a clear view which it's **committed** to, and isn't willing to compromise (i.e. the minority isn't willing to give in to the pressure to conform).

3) This creates a **conflict** — when you're faced with a consistent minority you have to seriously consider whether they might be right, and if you should change your view. Moscovici called this the **validation process**.

4) If there's no reason to **dismiss** the minority view (there doesn't seem to be an error in their perception or reasoning, they're not acting out of self-interest, and so on), then you begin to see things as the **minority** does.

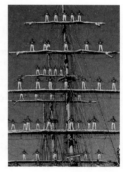

The longer Ron stayed on the mast, the more people joined him.

Social Impact Theory Outlines Three **Influential Factors**

Latané and Wolf's **social impact theory** (1981) argued that social influence occurs when the **combined** effects of **three factors** are significant enough:

1) **Strength** — how powerful, knowledgeable, and consistent the group appear to be.

2) **Numbers** — how many people are in the group.

3) **Immediacy** — how close the source of influence is to you (physically, or in terms of a relationship).

Latané and Wolf's theory says that **minority influence** happens through the same process as **majority influence** — it's just the **balance** of factors that create the social influence that's different.

The number of people in a minority is relatively small, but if the minority has strength and immediacy they can still exert **social influence** — a majority doesn't need as much strength or immediacy, because they have the numbers.

Lots of studies have provided **support** for social impact theory. However, Mullen (1985) conducted a **meta-analysis** of studies investigating social impact theory and found that lots of them relied on **self report** rather than observable behaviour. He argued that support for social impact theory could actually be a result of **demand characteristics** (see page 89). A **field experiment** by Sedikides and Jackson (1990) did provide support for social impact theory though, which contradicts Mullen's findings.

Minority Influence and Social Change

Minorities Can Become Majorities through the Snowball Effect

Whatever the process (conversion theory or social impact theory), minority influence is necessary for **social change** to take place...

1) If some people in a group start to agree with a minority view then the minority becomes more **influential**. This results in more and more people converting to the minority view. Eventually the minority becomes a majority. **Van Avermaet (1996)** described this as the **snowball effect**.

2) For this to happen people need to go from **privately** accepting the minority view to **publicly** expressing it.

3) One explanation of why this might happen is **social cryptoamnesia** — this means public opinion changes gradually over time, until the minority view is **accepted as the norm**, but people forget where the view originally came from.

Minorities Can Cause Social Change

There are many examples in history of things changing because the ideas of a few have taken hold. Try these for starters:

Martin Luther King

1) In the 1950s in America, black people did not have the same **rights** as white people. For example, in parts of America, buses were **segregated** and black people had to give up their seats to white people.

2) **Reverend Martin Luther King** challenged the views of the majority to bring about **political and social rights** for black people. He and other activists used **peaceful** protests like marches and sit-ins. This was known as the **Civil Rights Movement**. His ideas were so unpopular that during this time his home was bombed by activists, he was subjected to personal abuse, and he was **arrested**.

3) In the end though, the actions of civil rights activists influenced the **majority**. Nowadays there are **laws** that ensure people are given equal rights regardless of racial origin, and in 1964 Martin Luther King was awarded the **Nobel Peace Prize**.

Suzie was confident that it was only a matter of time before everyone started dressing like her.

Gay Rights Movements

1) Homosexuality used to be **illegal** in the UK. It was **decriminalised** in England and Wales in 1967 — but the age of consent was 21 (higher than for heterosexual people) and homosexuals were still treated **negatively**.

2) Over the last few decades, there have been moves towards equality as a result of **Gay Rights Movements**. These **minorities** have successfully **changed attitudes**. For example, the Equality Act (Sexual Orientation) 2007 made it **illegal to discriminate** against gay men and women in the provision of goods and services, and **same-sex marriage** was legalised in the UK in 2014.

Practice Questions

Q1 According to Moscovici et al's (1969) study, how does consistency affect minority influence?

Q2 What is social cryptoamnesia?

Exam Questions

Q1 Outline and evaluate one study into minority influence.   [8 marks]

Q2 Discuss how social influence can lead to social change.   [12 marks]

The times they are a-changing...

So minority influence can be a big deal. Here's an example: I think you should learn the stuff on this page. Most people probably don't agree — but you will, won't you? I've really got under your skin, haven't I? Power to the minority!

Types of Memory

Cognitive psychologists are interested in mental processes, and one of their big areas of research is memory.

Memory is a **Process** in Which Information is **Retained** About the Past

Most psychologists agree that there are three types of memory — the **sensory register**, **short-term memory (STM)** and **long-term memory (LTM)**. The three memory stores differ in **duration** (how long a memory lasts), **capacity** (how much can be held in the memory) and **coding** (how information is stored, creating a 'trace').

Sensory Register

1) The sensory register **temporarily** stores information from our **senses** (sight, sound, touch, taste and smell) — it's constantly receiving information from around us.

2) Unless we pay attention to it, it disappears quickly through **spontaneous decay** — the trace just fades.

3) The **sensory register** has a **limited capacity**, and a **very limited duration** (i.e. we can remember a little information for a very short time).

4) Information is **coded** depending on the sense that has picked it up — e.g. **visual**, **auditory** or **tactile**.

Short-Term Memory

1) **Short-term memory** has a **limited capacity** and a **limited duration** (i.e. we can remember a little information for a short time).

2) **Coding** is usually **acoustic** (sound).

Long-Term Memory

1) **Long-term memory** has a pretty much **unlimited capacity** and is theoretically **permanent** (i.e. it can hold lots of information forever). **Coding** is usually **semantic** (the meaning of the information).

2) There are different types of long-term memory:

- **Episodic memory** stores information about **events** that you've actually experienced, such as a concert or a visit to a restaurant. It can contain information about time and place, emotions you felt, and the details of what happened. These memories are **declarative** — this means they can be consciously recalled.

- **Semantic memory** stores **facts and knowledge** that we have learnt and can consciously recall, such as capital cities and word meanings. It doesn't contain details of the time or place where you learnt the information — it's simply the knowledge.

- **Procedural memory** stores the knowledge of how to do things, such as walking, swimming or playing the piano. This information **can't** be consciously recalled.

Studies Have Looked at the **Duration** of Memory

Sperling (1960) Investigated the Sensory Register Using Very Brief Displays

	Sperling (1960) — An investigation of the sensory register
Method:	In a **laboratory experiment**, participants were shown a grid with three rows of four letters for **50 milliseconds** (0.05 seconds). They then had to **immediately recall** either the **whole grid**, or a randomly chosen **row** indicated by a tone (high, medium or low) played straight after the grid was shown.
Results:	When participants had to recall the **whole grid**, they only managed to recall **four or five letters** on average. When a particular **row** was indicated, participants could recall an average of **three items**, no matter which row had been selected.
Conclusion:	The participants didn't know which row was going to be selected, so it could be concluded that they would have been able to recall three items from **any** row, therefore almost the whole grid was held in their sensory register. They couldn't report the whole grid because the trace **faded** before they could finish recall.
Evaluation:	Because this was a laboratory experiment, it was highly scientific. The **variables** could be controlled, and it would be easy for someone to **replicate** the study. However, the **artificial** setting of the study means that it lacks **ecological validity** — people don't normally have to recall letters in response to a sound, so the results might not represent what would happen in the real world.

Types of Memory

Peterson and Peterson (1959) Investigated STM Using Trigrams

Peterson and Peterson (1959) — The duration of STM

Method: Participants were shown **nonsense trigrams** (3 random consonants, e.g. CVM) and asked to recall them after either 3, 6, 9, 12, 15 or 18 seconds. During the pause, they were asked to count backwards in threes from a given number. This was an '**interference task**' to prevent them from repeating the letters internally.

Results: After **3 seconds**, participants could recall about **80%** of trigrams correctly.
After **18 seconds**, only about **10%** were recalled correctly.

Conclusion: When rehearsal is prevented, **very little** can stay in STM for longer than about **18 seconds**.

Evaluation: The results are likely to be reliable — it's a **laboratory experiment** where the variables can be tightly controlled. However, nonsense trigrams are artificial, so the study lacks **ecological validity** (see page 82 for more about reliability and validity). Meaningful or 'real-life' memories may last longer in STM. Only one type of **stimulus** was used — the duration of STM may depend on the type of stimulus. Also, each participant saw **many different trigrams**. This could have led to confusion, meaning that the first trigram was the only realistic trial.

Bahrick et al (1975) Investigated LTM in a Natural Setting

Bahrick et al (1975) — Very long-term memories (VLTMs)

Method: 392 people were asked to list the names of their ex-classmates. (This is called a '**free-recall test**'.) They were then shown photos and asked to recall the names of the people shown (**photo-recognition test**) or given names and asked to match them to a photo of the classmate (**name-recognition test**).

Results: Within 15 years of leaving school, participants could **recognise** about **90%** of names and faces. They were about **60%** accurate on **free recall**. After 30 years, **free recall** had declined to about **30%** accuracy. After 48 years, name-recognition was about **80%** accurate, and photo-recognition about **40%** accurate.

Conclusion: The study is evidence of **VLTMs** in a '**real-life**' setting. Recognition is better than recall, so there may be a huge store of information, but it's not always easy to **access** all of it — you just need help to get to it.

Evaluation: This was a field experiment and so had **high ecological validity**. However in a 'real-life' study like this, it's hard to **control** all the variables, making these findings less reliable — there's no way of knowing exactly **why** information was recalled well. It showed better recall than other studies on LTM, but this may be because **meaningful** information is stored better. This type of information could be rehearsed (if you're still in touch with classmates, or if you talk to friends about memories of classmates), increasing the rate of recall. This means that the results can't be generalised to other types of information held in LTM.

Studies Have Looked at the **Capacity** of Memory

STM and LTM Have Very **Different Capacities**

Jacobs (1887) — The capacity of STM

Method: Participants were presented with a string of letters or digits. They had to repeat them back in the same order. The number of digits or letters increased until the participant failed to recall the sequence correctly.

Results: The majority of the time, participants recalled about **9 digits** and about **7 letters**. This capacity increased with **age** during childhood.

Conclusion: Based on the range of results, Jacobs concluded that STM has a **limited storage capacity** of **5-9 items**. Individual differences were found, such as STM increasing with age, possibly due to use of memory techniques such as **chunking** (see the next page). Digits may have been easier to recall as there were only 10 different digits to remember, compared to 26 letters.

Evaluation: Jacobs' research is **artificial** and **lacks ecological validity** — it's not something you'd do in real life. Meaningful information may be recalled better, perhaps showing STM to have an even greater capacity. Also, the previous sequences recalled by the participants might have confused them on future trials.

Types of Memory

Miller Reviewed Research into the **Capacity of STM**

1) **Miller (1956)** reviewed research into the capacity of STM.
   He found that people can remember about seven items.

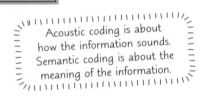
People find numbers easier to remember than letters.

2) He argued that the capacity of STM is **seven, plus or minus two** — 'Miller's magic number'.

3) He suggested that we use '**chunking**' to combine individual letters or numbers into larger, more meaningful units.

> For example, **2,0,0,3,1,9,8,7** is about all the digits STM can hold.
> 'Chunked' into the meaningful recent years of **2003** and **1987**, it's much easier to remember.

STM could probably hold about seven such pieces of chunked information, increasing STM's capacity.

Coding is About the Way Information is **Stored** in Memory

1) In **STM**, we sometimes try to keep information active by repeating it to ourselves. This means it generally involves **acoustic** coding.

2) In **LTM**, coding is generally **semantic** — it's more useful to code words in terms of their meaning, rather than what they sound or look like (although coding in LTM **can** also be visual or acoustic).

> Acoustic coding is about how the information sounds. Semantic coding is about the meaning of the information.

Baddeley (1966) — Investigating coding in STM and LTM

Method:	Participants were given four sets of words that were either **acoustically similar** (e.g. man, mad, mat), **acoustically dissimilar** (e.g. pit, cow, bar), **semantically similar** (e.g. big, large, huge) or **semantically dissimilar** (e.g. good, hot, pig). The experiment used an **independent groups** design (see page 80) — participants were asked to recall the words either immediately or following a 20-minute task.
Results:	Participants had problems recalling acoustically similar words when recalling the word list immediately (from **STM**). If recalling after an interval (from **LTM**), they had problems with semantically similar words.
Conclusion:	The patterns of confusion between similar words suggest that **LTM** is more likely to rely on **semantic** coding and **STM** on **acoustic** coding.
Evaluation:	This is another study that **lacks ecological validity**. Also, there are **other types** of LTM (e.g. episodic memory, procedural memory) and **other methods** of coding (e.g. visual) which this experiment doesn't consider. The experiment used an **independent groups** design, so there wasn't any control over participant variables.

Practice Questions

Q1 What is coding?

Q2 Outline Sperling's (1960) study.

Q3 What is Miller's magic number?

Exam Questions

Q1 Identify and outline **two** types of long-term memory. [4 marks]

Q2 Outline and evaluate research into the differences between short-term and long-term memory. [12 marks]

Remember the days when you didn't have to remember stuff like this...

So already you can probably see that there's more to memory than what you can remember and what you can't. But don't worry — if... oh, hang on, what was I saying... Ah yes, if you make sure you know what the sensory register, short-term memory and long-term memory are, and how they differ, then you'll be on the road to collecting marks.

Models of Memory

Before you start reading this page, make sure you've got to grips with what short-term memory, long-term memory and the sensory register are. If you've even got the slightest niggling doubt, head back to page 14 to remind yourself.

Atkinson and Shiffrin (1968) Created the *Multi-Store Model*

1) The multi-store model proposes that memory consists of three stores — a **sensory register**, a **short-term store** and a **long-term store**, and information has to move through these stores to become a memory.

2) Information from our environment (e.g. visual or auditory) initially goes into the **sensory register**. You don't really notice much of this stuff. However, if you pay attention to it, or think about it, the information will pass into **short-term memory**.

3) Short-term memory has a **finite** capacity and duration. But if information is processed further (rehearsed) then it can be transferred to **long-term memory**. In theory, the information can then remain there forever. (Unless you really, really need to remember it, in which case it'll probably stay there until something more interesting comes along, like a bee or a cloud.)

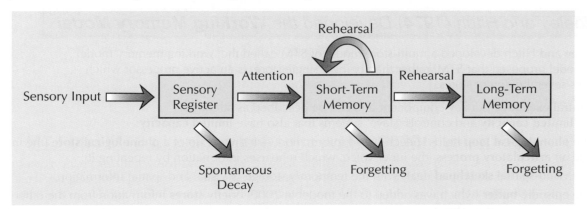

Many Studies *Support* the Multi-Store Model...

Several studies have been carried out that show that memory is made up of separate stores.

1) The **Primacy Effect** — Research shows that participants are able to recall the first few items of a list better than those from the middle. The multi-store model explains this because **earlier** items will have been **rehearsed** better and transferred to **LTM**. If rehearsal is prevented by an **interference task**, the effect disappears.

2) The **Recency Effect** — Participants also tend to remember the **last few** items better than those from the middle of the list. As STM has a capacity of around 7 items, the words in the middle of the list, if not rehearsed, are **displaced** from STM by the last few words heard. These last words are still in **STM** at the end of the experiment and can be **recalled**.

3) People with **Korsakoff's Syndrome** (amnesia that's mostly caused by chronic alcoholism) provide support for the model. They can recall the **last** items in a list (unimpaired recency effect), suggesting an unaffected **STM**. However, their **LTM** is very poor. This supports the model by showing that STM and LTM are **separate stores**.

4) **Milner et al (1957)** carried out a **case study** into a patient called HM who had suffered from severe and frequent epilepsy. His seizures were based in a brain structure called the hippocampus. Doctors decided to surgically remove part of the brain around this area. The operation reduced his epilepsy, but led to him suffering **memory loss**. He could still form **short-term memories**, but was unable to form **new long-term memories**. This case study supports the idea that different types of memory are **separate systems** in the brain.

Models of Memory

...But There Are Also Many **Limitations** of the Model

Although there's lots of support for the model, there's plenty of criticism too.

1) In the model, information is transferred from the STM to LTM through **rehearsal**. But in **real life** people don't always spend time rehearsing, yet they still transfer information into LTM. Rehearsal is not always needed for information to be stored and some items can't be rehearsed, e.g. smells.

2) The model is **oversimplified**. It assumes there is only one long-term store and one short-term store. This has been disproved by evidence from **brain damaged** patients, suggesting several **different** short-term stores, and other evidence suggesting different long-term stores.

Baddeley and Hitch (1974) Developed the **Working Memory Model**

Baddeley and Hitch developed a multi-store model of STM called the 'working memory model'. Their model proposed that STM, rather than being a single store, is an active processor which contains several different stores.

The **central executive** is a key component and can be described as attention. It has a **limited capacity** and controls 'slave' systems that also have **limited capacity**:

1) The **phonological loop** holds speech-based information — it's made up of a **phonological store** (the inner ear) and an **articulatory process** (the inner voice, which rehearses information by repeating it).

2) The **visuo-spatial sketchpad** deals with the temporary storage of visual and spatial information.

3) The **episodic buffer** (which was added to the model in 2000) briefly **stores** information from the other subsystems and **integrates** it together, along with information from LTM, to make complete scenes or '**episodes**'.

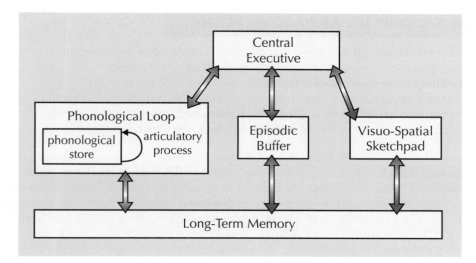

The **Working Memory Model** Came From **Experimental Evidence**

Baddeley and Hitch based their model on results from studies that used '**interference tasks**':

1) If participants are asked to perform two tasks simultaneously that use the **same system**, their performance will be **affected** — e.g. saying 'the the the' while silently reading something is very difficult.

2) According to the working memory model, both these tasks use the **phonological loop**. This has **limited capacity**, so it can't cope with both tasks. Performance on one, or both tasks, will be affected.

3) However, if the two tasks involve **different systems**, performance **isn't affected** on either task (e.g. saying 'the the the' whilst tracking a moving object).

Models of Memory

As Usual the Model has **Strengths**...

1) **Shallice and Warrington (1974)** found **support** for the working memory model through their case study of KF.

> **KF** was a brain-damaged patient who had an impaired STM. His problem was with immediate recall of words presented **verbally**, but not with visual information. This suggested he had an **impaired articulatory loop** but an intact visuo-spatial sketchpad, therefore providing evidence for the working memory model's view of STM. This finding could not have been explained using the multi-store model of memory, which proposed that short-term memory was just one system.

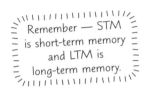
Remember — STM is short-term memory and LTM is long-term memory.

2) **Gathercole and Baddeley (1993)** reported on a laboratory study which **supports** the model:

> Participants were split into **two groups**. All of the participants had to carry out a task where they had to follow a moving spot of light. This would use the **visuo-spatial sketchpad**. At the same time, one group of participants also had to describe the angles on a letter — another task involving the **visuo-spatial sketchpad**. The other group of participants were given a second task that would use the **phonological loop** — they had to do a **verbal** task whilst following the light. Gathercole and Baddeley found that performance was much **better** in the participants doing tasks which used **separate systems**.

3) The model has **less emphasis** on **rehearsal** than the multi-store model of memory. Rather than being the key process, rehearsal is just **one possible** process in the working memory model. This can therefore help to explain why, in real life, some things end up in our long-term memory even though we haven't rehearsed them — it suggests that other processes are at work.

... and **Weaknesses**

The working memory model is currently the main model of short-term memory, but some psychologists have **criticised** it. For example:

1) They think that Baddeley and Hitch's idea of a central executive is **simplistic** and **vague**. Their model doesn't really explain exactly what the central executive is, apart from being involved in attention. However, it's difficult to design tasks to test the central executive.

2) The model only explains how information is dealt with in **short-term memory**. It doesn't explain how information is **transferred** to long-term memory.

3) Much of the research which has supported the working memory model has been **laboratory studies**. This reduces the **ecological validity** of the evidence, as highly controlled studies might not be representative of what happens in the real world.

Practice Questions

Q1 What is the primacy effect?
Q2 Who came up with the working memory model?
Q3 How did the study of KF provide support for the working memory model?

Exam Questions

Q1 Which of these is **not** a component of the working memory model?
   A central executive   **B** phonological loop   **C** visuo-spatial sketchpad   **D** sensory register   [1 mark]

Q2 Describe and evaluate the multi-store model of memory.   [12 marks]

My friend does shoots for all the high street shops — she's a multi-store model...

These pages might not have the excitement factor of electric shocks and general nastiness, but it's good solid psychology, and I'm afraid you need to know it. As well as knowing their features, make sure you know the strengths and weaknesses of the models so that you can evaluate them. And have a few studies up your sleeve for support.

Forgetting

This page is all about why you can't remember the last page. Maybe you didn't rehearse it enough, or maybe you only looked at the letters instead of trying to understand the facts. Or maybe you spilt tea on it and couldn't read the words...

Forgetting *is When Learnt Information* Can't be Retrieved

1) Experiments on memory assume that if you **can't retrieve** a memory, it's forgotten.

2) Forgetting information from STM is thought to be down to an **availability problem** — the information is no longer available because of the **limited capacity** or the **limited duration** of STM. The information may have been **pushed out (displaced)** or simply have **faded away (decayed)**.

3) In **long-term memory** forgetting can be caused by **decay** (an availability problem), but it can also be because:

   - The information was stored, but is hard to **retrieve** — an **accessibility** problem,
     e.g. you read something once, a long time ago, and now need a lot of help to recall it.

   - The information is **confused** — there is an **interference** problem,
     e.g. two pieces of learnt information are too similar, and you can't tell them apart easily.

Interference *is One* Explanation *for* Forgetting

One theory about forgetting is that your **ability to remember** a particular thing you've learnt can be affected by having learnt something similar **before** or **since**. This is known as **interference** — there are two types:

Retroactive Interference

Retroactive interference is where **new information** interferes with the ability to recall **older information**.

> **Underwood and Postman (1960)** carried out a study which supported **retroactive interference**. In a lab experiment, participants were split into two groups. Both groups were given a list of **paired words** to learn, e.g. **cat–tree**. The experimental group was then given a **second list** of words to learn, where the **first** of the words in each pair was the **same** as in the first list, e.g. **cat–dirt**. The control group wasn't given a second word list. Both groups were then tested on their **recall** of the **first word list**, by being given the first word from each pair. Recall was better in the **control group**, suggesting that **retroactive interference** of the second word list had affected recall for the experimental group.

Proactive Interference

Proactive interference is where **older information** interferes with the ability to recall **new information**.

> **Underwood (1957)** studied **proactive interference** by looking at the results of studies into forgetting over a 24-hour period. He found that if people had previously learnt **15 or more word lists** during the same experiment, a day later their recall of the last word list was around **20%**. If they **hadn't** learnt any earlier lists, recall a day later was around **80%**. Underwood concluded that **proactive interference** from the earlier lists had affected the participants' ability to remember later ones.

Jasper couldn't quite recall what his mother had told him about these things.

The Interference Theory Has Strengths *and* Weaknesses

1) Proactive and retroactive interference are **supported** by loads and loads of **studies**, many of which were highly controlled **laboratory experiments**.

2) As well as in laboratory experiments, there is evidence for interference existing in **real-world settings** too. For example, you might struggle to remember your French vocabulary if you later start learning German.

3) However, interference effects seem much greater in **artificial** laboratory settings than they do in real life, so it may not be **as strong** a theory as once thought.

4) The theory gives us an explanation for **why** we forget, but it doesn't go into the cognitive or biological **processes** involved — it doesn't fully explain why or how interference happens.

Forgetting

Recall *Can Depend on Getting the Right* Cues

Another theory of memory states that being able to recall a piece of information depends on getting the **right cue**. In this theory, forgetting is treated as a **retrieval failure** — the information still exists in memory but it isn't **accessible**.

We have more chance of retrieving the memory if the **cue** is **appropriate**. Cues can be **internal** (e.g. your mood) or **external** (e.g. context, like surroundings, situation, etc.). We remember more if we are in the same **context/mood** as we were in when we coded the information originally. This is known as **cue-dependent learning**.

	Tulving and Psotka (1971) — Forgetting in LTM
Method:	Tulving and Psotka compared the theories of **interference** and **cue-dependent forgetting**.
	Each participant was given either 1, 2, 3, 4, 5 or 6 lists of 24 words. Each list was divided into 6 categories of 4 words. Words were presented in category order, e.g. all animals, then all trees etc. After the lists were presented, in one condition, participants had to simply recall all the words — **total free recall**. In another condition, participants were given all the category names and had to try to recall words from the list — **free cued recall**.
Results:	In the **total free recall** condition, there seemed to be evidence of **retroactive** interference. Participants with 1 or 2 lists to remember had higher recall than those with more lists to remember, suggesting the later lists were **interfering** with remembering the earlier lists.
	However, in the **cued recall** test, the effects of retroactive interference **disappeared**. It didn't matter how many lists a participant had — recall was still the same for each list (about **70%**).
Conclusion:	The results suggest that interference had not caused forgetting. Because the memories became accessible if a cue was used, it showed that they were available, but just inaccessible. Therefore, the forgetting shown in the total free recall condition was **cue-dependent forgetting**.
Evaluation:	Tulving and Psotka's study was a **laboratory experiment** so will have been highly **controlled**, reducing the effect of **extraneous variables** (page 79). However, laboratory experiments lack **ecological validity** as the setting and task are **artificial**. The study only tested memory of words, so the results can't reliably be **generalised** to information of other types.

As usual, the theory has strengths and weaknesses:

1) Cue-dependent forgetting is thought to be the best explanation of forgetting in LTM, as it has the **strongest** evidence. Most forgetting is seen to be caused by **retrieval failure**. This means that virtually all memory we have is available in LTM — we just need the right cue to be able to access it.

2) However, the evidence is **artificial** (e.g. recalling word lists), lacking meaning in the real world. Also, it would be difficult, if not impossible, to test whether all information in LTM is accessible and available, and just waiting for the right cue.

3) The theory might not explain **all types** of memory. For example, cues might not be relevant to procedural memory (see page 14), such as remembering how to ride a bike or play a musical instrument.

Practice Questions

Q1 What is retroactive interference?
Q2 What is proactive interference?
Q3 Give one weakness of the interference theory of forgetting.

Exam Question

Q1 In a study, participants learned a word list in either a room painted red or a room painted yellow.
They were then tested either in the same room, or in the other coloured room.
Recall was better when participants were tested in the same room that they had learned in.
Outline and evaluate a theory of forgetting that could explain why this occurred.   [8 marks]

Remember, remember the 5th of October...

Make up some word lists and get your friends to read them. Give them an interference task, then test them. I'm always doing experiments on my friends... well, I was until that incident with the misplaced electrode anyway.

Eyewitness Testimony

If you witness a crime or an accident, you might have to report what you saw, and your version of events could be crucial in prosecuting someone... But your memory isn't as accurate as you might think...

Eyewitness Testimony Can Be **Inaccurate** and **Distorted**

1) **Eyewitness testimony** (EWT) is the **evidence** provided by people who **witnessed** a particular event or crime. It relies on **recall** from memory.

2) EWT includes, for example, **descriptions** of criminals (e.g. hair colour, height) and crime scenes (e.g. time, date, location).

3) Witnesses are often **inaccurate** in their recollection of events and the people involved. As you can probably imagine, this has important implications when it comes to police interviews.

4) Many cognitive psychologists focus on working out what **factors** affect the accuracy of eyewitness testimony, and how accuracy can be **improved** in interviews.

Eyewitness Testimony Can Be Affected by **Misleading Information**

Loftus and Palmer (1974) investigated how EWT can be **distorted**.
They used **leading questions**, where a certain answer is implied in the question.

For example, the question, "How much will prices go up next year?" is leading, because it implies that prices **will** go up. A better question would be, "What do you think will happen to prices next year?"

Loftus and Palmer (1974) — A study into eyewitness testimony

Loftus and Palmer carried out two experiments in their study.

Experiment 1:

Method:	Participants were shown a film of a multiple car crash. They were then asked a series of questions including 'How fast do you think the cars were going when they **hit**?' In different conditions, the word 'hit' was replaced with '**smashed**', '**collided**', '**bumped**' or '**contacted**'.
Results:	Participants given the word '**smashed**' estimated the **highest speed** (an average of 41 mph); those given the word '**contacted**' gave the **lowest** estimate (an average of 32 mph).

Experiment 2:

Method:	The participants were split into three groups. One group was given the verb 'smashed', another 'hit', and the third, control group wasn't given any indication of the vehicles' speed. A week later, the participants were asked '**Did you see any broken glass?**'.
Results:	Although there was no broken glass in the film, participants were more likely to say that they'd seen broken glass in the '**smashed**' condition than any other.
Conclusion:	**Leading questions** can affect the **accuracy** of people's memories of an event.
Evaluation:	This has implications for questions in **police interviews**. However, this was an artificial experiment — watching a video is not as **emotionally arousing** as a real-life event, which potentially affects recall. In fact, a later study found that participants who thought they'd witnessed a **real** robbery could give an **accurate** description of the robber. The experimental design might lead to **demand characteristics**, where the results are skewed because of the participants' expectations about the purposes of the experiment. For example, the leading questions might have given participants **clues** about the nature of the experiment (e.g. they could have realised that the experiment was about susceptibility to leading questions), and so participants might have acted accordingly. This would have reduced the **validity** and **reliability** of the experiment.

Eyewitness Testimony

Loftus and Zanni (1975) also Looked at Leading Questions

Loftus and Zanni (1975) investigated how altering the wording of a question can produce a **leading question** that can distort EWT.

Loftus and Zanni (1975) — A study into leading questions

Method:	Participants were shown a film of a car crash. They were then asked either 'Did you see **the** broken headlight?' or 'Did you see **a** broken headlight?'. There was no broken headlight shown in the film.
Results:	17% of those asked about 'the' broken headlight claimed they saw one, compared to 7% in the group asked about 'a' broken headlight.
Conclusion:	The simple use of the word '**the**' is enough to affect the accuracy of people's memories of an event.
Evaluation:	Like the study by Loftus and Palmer (previous page), this study has implications for eyewitness testimony. This study was a **laboratory study**, which made it possible to control any **extraneous variables** (p.79) This means it's possible to establish **cause and effect**. However, the study was **artificial** (participants were shown a film of a car crash, not an actual car crash), so the study lacked **ecological validity**.

Post-Event Discussion Can Affect the Accuracy of Recall

Studies where a confederate has been used to feed other participants with **misleading post-event information** have shown that this can affect recall. For example:

Shaw et al (1997) paired participants with a confederate (who pretended to be another participant). The pairs were shown videos of a **staged robbery** and were interviewed together afterwards. The participant and the confederate alternated who answered the questions first. When the **participant** responded **first**, recall was accurate **58%** of the time. When the **confederate** answered first and gave **accurate** answers, the recall of the participants was **67%**. If the confederate gave **inaccurate** answers, correct recall for the participants fell to **42%**.

If the misleading information is received through a **conversation**, the effects can be just as big, if not bigger. For example:

Gabbert et al's (2004) study involved two groups of participants — young adults (17-33 years old) and older adults (58-80 years old). Both groups watched a **staged crime** and were then exposed to misleading information in one of two ways — through **conversation** with a confederate who was pretending to be another participant, or reading a **written report** of the crime, supposedly written by another participant. The participants were then given a recall test about the event they'd witnessed. It was found that both groups of adults were more likely to report inaccurate information after a **conversation** with a confederate than after reading the report.

Practice Questions

Q1 What is eyewitness testimony?
Q2 What are leading questions?
Q3 What leading question was used in Loftus and Zanni's (1975) study?
Q4 How can post-event discussion affect the accuracy of recall?

Exam Question

Q1 Outline and evaluate research into the effect of misleading information on eyewitness testimony. [8 marks]

Do you remember the fun time you had reading this page...?*

If you witness something dead important, remember that not everything you think you remember did definitely happen. Leading questions can, for example, mislead people into thinking they saw something they didn't. So little brother, what colour was the dog that you saw eating all Mum's luxury chocolate biscuits? Burp.

Eyewitness Testimony

The *Age* of the *Witness* Can Affect the *Accuracy of Eyewitness Testimony*

Studies have shown that the **age** of the witness is a factor in whether they're affected by leading questions.

Valentine and Coxon (1997) — The effect of age on EWT

Method:	3 groups of participants (children, young adults and elderly people) watched a video of a kidnapping. They were then asked a series of leading and non-leading questions about what they had seen.
Results:	Both the elderly people and the children gave more incorrect answers to non-leading questions. Children were misled more by leading questions than adults or the elderly.
Conclusion:	Age has an effect on the accuracy of eyewitness testimony.
Evaluation:	This has **implications** in law when children or elderly people are questioned. However, the experiment was **artificial** and so wasn't as emotionally arousing as the same situation would have been in real life — the study **lacks ecological validity**. The results may only show how well people remember things from **TV**, rather than showing the accuracy of memories of real-life situations.

Anxiety Can Affect *Focus*

Psychologists tend to believe that **small increases** in anxiety and arousal may **increase the accuracy** of memory, but **high levels** have a **negative effect** on accuracy.

In **violent crimes** (where anxiety and arousal are likely to be high), the witness may focus on **central details** (e.g. a weapon) and neglect other peripheral details (e.g. what the criminal was wearing).

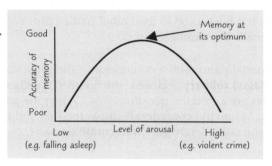

Eyewitnesses recall seeing fair weather and blue skies, but nothing else remarkable.

Loftus (1979) — Weapon focus in EWT

Method:	In a study with an **independent groups** design, participants heard a discussion in a nearby room. In one condition, a man came out of the room with a pen and grease on his hands. In the second condition, the man came out carrying a knife covered in blood. Participants were asked to identify the man from 50 photographs.
Results:	Participants in condition 1 were 49% accurate. Only 33% of the participants in condition 2 were correct.
Conclusion:	When anxious and aroused, witnesses focus on a weapon at the expense of other details.
Evaluation:	The study has **high ecological validity**, as the participants weren't aware that the study was staged. However, this means that there are also **ethical** considerations, as participants could have been very distressed at the sight of the man with the knife.

Misleading Questions and Anxiety *Don't Always* Affect EWT

1) A **field study** by **Yuille and Cutshall (1986)** showed that witnesses of a **real** incident (a gun shooting) had **remarkably accurate memories** of the event.

2) A thief was shot and killed by police and witnesses were interviewed. Thirteen of them were invited to be **re-interviewed five months later**. Recall was found to be **highly accurate**, even after this time period.

3) The researchers had included two **misleading questions** in the study but these were found to have **no effect** on the subjects' answers.

4) This study had **high ecological validity** as it was based on a real-life event. However, the witnesses who experienced the **highest levels of stress** were also **closest** to the event — it's difficult to determine whether **proximity** or **stress** contributed to the accuracy of their recall.

Eyewitness Testimony

The **Cognitive Interview** was Developed to **Increase Accuracy**

Cognitive psychologists have played a big part in helping to **increase the accuracy** of eyewitness testimony. As you've seen, research shows that the accuracy of eyewitness testimony is affected by many factors. The **cognitive interview technique (CIT)** was developed by **Geiselman et al (1984)** to try to increase the accuracy of witnesses' recall of events during police questioning.

Here's basically what happens in cognitive interviews:

1) The interviewer tries to make the witness **relaxed** and tailors his/her **language** to suit the witness.
2) The witness mentally recreates the **environmental context** (e.g. sights and sounds) and **internal context** (e.g. mood) of the crime scene.
3) The witness reports absolutely **everything** that they can remember about the crime, even if it feels irrelevant.
4) The witness is asked to recall details of the crime in **different orders**.
5) The witness is asked to recall the event from various **different perspectives**, e.g. from the eyes of other witnesses.
6) The interviewer avoids any **judgemental** and **personal comments**.

There is **Research** to **Support** the Cognitive Interview

Research has shown that people interviewed with the cognitive interview technique are much more **accurate** in their recall of events. For example:

Geiselman et al (1986) — The effect of the cognitive interview

Method:	In a staged situation, an intruder carrying a **blue** rucksack entered a classroom and stole a slide projector. Two days later, participants were questioned about the event. The study used an **independent groups** design — participants were either questioned using a standard interview procedure or the cognitive interview technique. Early in the questioning, participants were asked 'Was the guy with the **green** backpack nervous?'. Later in the interview, participants were asked what colour the man's rucksack was.
Results:	Participants in the cognitive interview condition were less likely to recall the rucksack as being green than those in the standard interview condition.
Conclusion:	The cognitive interview technique **reduces the effect of leading questions**.
Evaluation:	The experiment was conducted as though a real crime had taken place in the classroom — it had **high ecological validity**. The experiment used an **independent groups** design. The disadvantage of this is that the participants in the cognitive interview condition could have been naturally less susceptible to leading questions than the other group (due to individual differences).

The CIT has been shown to increase the accuracy of EWT. This means the police can work more efficiently, so public money is better spent, which in turn is beneficial for the economy.

Practice Questions

Q1 What did Valentine and Coxon's (1997) study show about the effect of age on eyewitness testimony?

Q2 What did the study by Yuille and Cutshall (1986) show about the effect of misleading questions on recall?

Q3 Who developed the cognitive interview technique?

Exam Questions

Q1 Briefly outline the effect that anxiety can have on the accuracy of eyewitness testimony. [4 marks]

Q2 Outline the techniques used in a cognitive interview. [4 marks]

A tall, thin man, quite short, with black, fair hair — great fat bloke she was...

Well, now I haven't a clue what I've really experienced in my life. Did that man I saw shoplifting really have stubble, scars and a ripped leather jacket, or is that just my shoplifter stereotype kicking in? In fact, come to think of it, I couldn't actually tell you whether my granny has a hairy chin or not. I think she does, but then I think all grannies do...

Attachment

These pages deal with the different features of attachments and how they develop between infants and their carers.
Simple eh — you'd think, but this is psychology after all...

Attachment is a Strong **Emotional Bond**

Attachment is a close emotional relationship between an infant and their caregiver.
'Securely attached' infants will show a desire to be **close** to their **primary caregiver** (usually their biological mother).
They'll show **distress** when they're **separated**, and **pleasure** when they're **reunited**.

Features of **Caregiver-Infant** Interaction

There are common **caregiver-infant interactions** which are seen in attachments.
These are thought to be involved in **developing** and **maintaining** the attachment.

1) **Sensitive responsiveness** — The caregiver responds appropriately to signals from the infant.

2) **Imitation** — The infant copies the caregiver's actions and behaviour. For example, Meltzoff and Moore (1977) found that infants between 2 and 3 weeks of age appeared to imitate the facial expressions and hand movements of the experimenter.

3) **Interactional synchrony** — Infants react in time with the caregiver's speech, resulting in a 'conversation dance'. **Condon and Sander (1974)** provided evidence for this concept, by showing how babies do appear to move in time with adult conversations.

4) **Reciprocity/turn-taking** — Interaction flows back and forth between the caregiver and infant.

5) **Motherese** — The slow, high-pitched way of speaking to infants. However, there is no evidence that this influences the strength of an attachment between parent and infant.

Baby Juanita took 'imitating Mummy' quite literally.

Schaffer Identified **Stages** in Attachment Formation

1) The **pre-attachment (or asocial) phase** — During the first **0 to 3 months** of life, the baby learns to **separate** people from objects but doesn't have any strong preferences about who cares for it.

2) The **indiscriminate (or diffuse) attachment phase** — Between **6 weeks and seven months** the infant starts to clearly **distinguish** and **recognise** different people, smiling more at people it knows than at strangers. However, there are still no strong preferences about who cares for it.

3) The **discriminate (or single) attachment phase** — From **seven to eleven months** the infant becomes able to form a **strong attachment** with an **individual**. This is shown by being content when that person is around, distressed when they leave and happy when they return. It may be scared of strangers and avoid them.

4) The **multiple attachment phase** — From about **nine months** the infant can form **attachments to many different people**. Some attachments may be stronger than others and have **different functions**, e.g. for play or comfort, but there doesn't seem to be a limit to the number of attachments it can make. Although Schaffer found that after 18 months, approximately **32%** of babies had **at least five** attachments, the original attachment is still the strongest.

Schaffer and Emerson (1964) — Evidence for attachment stages

Method:	60 babies were observed in their homes in Glasgow every four weeks from birth to about 18 months. Interviews were also conducted with their families.
Results:	Schaffer's stages of attachment formation were found to occur. Also, at 8 months of age about 50 of the infants had more than one attachment. About 20 of them either had no attachment with their mother or had a stronger attachment with someone else, even though the mother was always the main carer.
Conclusion:	Infants form attachments in **stages** and can eventually attach to **many people**. **Quality of care** is important in forming attachments, so the infant may not attach to their mother if other people respond more accurately to its signals.

Attachment

Evaluation of Schaffer and Emerson (1964)

There is now a lot of evidence to support Schaffer and Emerson's results and their stages of attachment formation, but there are also criticisms of the study. For example, Schaffer and Emerson used a **limited sample**, and evidence from interviews and observations may be **biased** and **unreliable**.

Additionally, there are some cross-cultural differences that should be considered. **Tronick et al (1992)** found that infants in Zaire had a strong attachment with their mother by six months of age but didn't have strong attachments with others, even though they had several carers.

The **Father** Plays an Important **Role** Too

Schaffer and Emerson (1964) found that the attachment between caregiver and infant varied across the infants. Their **mother** was the primary attachment for only **half** of the infants. A **third** of the infants preferred their **father**, whilst the **rest** had their strongest attachment with their **grandparents** or **siblings**.

A lot of the initial research into caregiver-infant attachment focused on the mother being the primary caregiver. But that ignores the role of the father.

- **Goodsell and Meldrum (2009)** conducted a large study into the relationship between infants and their fathers. They found that those with a secure attachment to their mother are also more likely to have a secure attachment to their father.

- **Ross et al (1975)** showed that the number of nappies a father changed was positively correlated to the strength of their attachment. This was supported by a study by **Caldera (2004)** who investigated 60 fathers and mothers and their 14-month-old infants. Caldera found that when the father was involved in care-giving activities, they were much more likely to develop a strong attachment with their child.

- But there is research which suggests the **role** a mother and father plays can be **different**. **Geiger (1996)** suggested that a mother's relationship is primarily **nurturing** and **caring**, but a father's relationship is more focused around **play**.

> As research has suggested that the primary caregiver can be the father, or even other substitutes, more mothers are returning to work after childbirth. This has a positive impact on the economy.

Practice Questions

Q1 What is 'attachment'?

Q2 What are the four stages of attachment described by Schaffer and Emerson (1964)?

Q3 Give one criticism of Schaffer and Emerson's (1964) research into the attachment of children.

Exam Questions

Q1 Read the extract, then answer the question that follows.

> At 6 months, whenever Selby got upset he was more than happy to be comforted by the nearest person. He smiled more at his mother, but was generally a very happy baby to be around. Three months later, he started to experience separation anxiety. He began to cry a lot when his mother left the room and wouldn't settle without his regular night-time routine.

Outline the **two** stages of attachment identified by Schaffer which are shown by Selby. [4 marks]

Q2 Which of these terms best describes the act of a child reacting in time with their caregiver's speech?
  A imitation   **B** motherese   **C** interactional synchrony   **D** sensitive responsiveness   [1 mark]

Multiple attachments sound great — if Mum says no, ask Dad...

There's lots of really useful info on these pages to get you excited about attachment. It's really relevant too. As times have started to change, and the role of the primary caregiver is shifting, it's a good idea to think about how fathers develop attachments with their children too. But, first things first — learn those stages of attachment formation.

Animal Studies of Attachment

Some psychologists have studied animals to try to uncover more about attachment. So next time you see a baby chicken hatching from an egg — be warned. It may become attached to you, and then there's no going back...

Lorenz Studied Imprinting in Geese

1) **Konrad Lorenz (1935)** found that geese automatically 'attach' to the first moving thing they see after hatching, and follow it everywhere (I bet this gets quite annoying). This is called **imprinting**.

2) He randomly divided a clutch of greylag goose eggs into two groups. He left one group with the mother and incubated the other eggs.

3) Lorenz observed that the goslings from the incubator eggs followed him around in exactly the same way that the goslings from the other eggs would follow their mother.

4) He put both sets of goslings together and observed that when they were released, the two groups quickly re-formed as the goslings went off in search of their respective 'mothers'. Both sets of goslings had imprinted on the first moving object that they had seen.

Lorenz wasn't an experienced father, but his geese loved him.

5) After further experiments, Lorenz determined that imprinting was most likely between 13 and 16 hours after hatching.

6) As such, he concluded that imprinting seems to occur during a **'critical period'**. It's a **fast**, **automatic** process.

7) He also noted that after this critical period, it was too late for the young birds ever to imprint.

8) It's unlikely to occur in humans. Our attachments take **longer** to develop and we don't automatically attach to particular things — quality care seems more important in human attachment formation. However, Bowlby's theory (page 30) is based on the same principles.

Harlow Showed That Comfort is Important in Attachment

Just because babies spend most of their time either eating or sleeping, it doesn't mean they automatically attach to the person who feeds them. Good quality interaction with the baby seems more important — the baby will attach to whoever is the most sensitive and loving. This is also shown in **Harlow's** study:

Harlow (1959) — The need for 'contact comfort'

Method:	Harlow aimed to find out whether baby monkeys would prefer a source of **food** or a source of **comfort** and **protection** as an attachment figure. In **laboratory experiments** rhesus monkeys were raised in isolation. They had two 'surrogate' mothers. One was made of wire mesh and contained a feeding bottle, the other was made of cloth but didn't contain a feeding bottle.
Results:	The monkeys spent most of their time clinging to the cloth surrogate and only used the wire surrogate to feed. The cloth surrogate seemed to give them **comfort** in new situations. When the monkeys grew up they showed signs of **social** and **emotional disturbance**. The females were bad mothers who were often violent towards their offspring.
Conclusion:	Infant monkeys formed more of an attachment with a figure that provided comfort and protection. Growing up in isolation affected their development.
Evaluation:	This was a **laboratory experiment**, so there was strict control of the variables. This means that it's unlikely the results were affected by an unknown variable. However, it can be argued that you can't **generalise** the results of this study to human beings, because humans and monkeys are **qualitatively different**. There were also **ethical problems** with this study — the monkeys were put in a stressful situation, and later they showed signs of being psychologically damaged by the experiment. Monkeys are social animals, so it was unfair to keep them in isolation. The fact that they were in isolation also means that the study lacked **ecological validity** — the monkeys weren't in their natural environment, so the results can't be reliably applied to real life. Laboratory experiments can usually be **replicated**, but ethical guidelines now in place mean that you couldn't repeat this study today to see whether you'd get the same results.

Animal Studies of Attachment

Harlow Continued His Research with Monkeys

Harlow's (1959) study concluded that rhesus monkeys developed **stronger** attachments with a cloth surrogate than a wire surrogate. He carried out further studies with different conditions.

Harlow's further research

Harlow and Zimmerman (1959) added in a **fearful** stimulus. When a fearful object (such as an oversized toy) was placed in the cage, the monkey would cling to the **cloth surrogate** first before exploring the object. Monkeys in cages with only a **wire surrogate** would remain frozen or run wildly around the cage. The researchers concluded that a **strong** attachment with a primary caregiver is therefore highly **important** in the development of an infant.

Harlow and Sumoi (1970) investigated other factors in generating a strong attachment. When they placed a cloth surrogate **with food** and a cloth surrogate **without food** in the cage, they found that the one **with food** was **preferred**. They concluded that **food** may still be a **significant** factor in developing attachments.

Psychologists Often Use Animals in Research

1) When animals are used in psychological research, the findings of the studies should be interpreted **carefully**. It is **hard to generalise** the findings from one species to another because the behaviour of an animal can often be very different to that of a human.

2) Lorenz used **precocial** species — these are species that have their eyes open and can walk right from birth. So they are very different from human infants, who cannot walk until a lot later.

> Precocial species want to stay close to the caregiver to avoid wandering off and getting eaten.

3) Although the results of animal studies might not always be generalisable to human populations, they can often **influence policies** and **theories** in different areas of research.

Researchers Have to Think About Ethics

> See pages 91-93 for more about ethics in general.

Although **animal studies** have provided **valuable information** for developmental research, there's debate about whether they're ethical or not.

Advantage — Some **research designs** couldn't have been conducted on humans ethically — e.g. Harlow's study of attachment, where young monkeys were separated from their mothers (see previous page).

Disadvantage — Some see it as **unethical** to inflict suffering on animals, especially when they can't give consent.

Practice Questions

Q1 What species did Lorenz (1935) use in his research on attachment?

Q2 What did Lorenz (1935) conclude from his study?

Q3 Why might researchers choose to use animals in their studies?

Exam Questions

Q1 Outline Lorenz's research investigating attachment.	[4 marks]
Q2 a) Outline Harlow's study into attachment.	[4 marks]
b) Evaluate the methodology Harlow used.	[4 marks]

Monkey lovin'...

Hanging around a pond waiting for the geese to hatch seems like a nice idea. I'd love to have some instant gosling children following me round. But I guess it wouldn't be so much fun when you have to regurgitate worms into their beaks at four in the morning. Then they break your arm with their wings. Or is that swans...

Explanations of Attachment

There are several different theories of attachment, from learning theory to Bowlby's monotropic theory.
Take a look at these two pages to learn all about them. It's exciting stuff. Really, it is.

Learning Theory Links Attachment to Pleasure

Learning theory is also known as the **behaviourist theory**, and focuses on the baby wanting its needs fulfilled.
Conditioning is given as an explanation for how attachments form.

See pages 42-47 for loads more on learning theory.

Classical Conditioning. This is about learning **associations** between different things in our environment. Getting food naturally gives the baby **pleasure**. The baby's desire for food is fulfilled whenever its mother is around to feed it. So an **association is formed between mother and food**. So, whenever its mother is around, the baby will feel pleasure — i.e. 'attachment'.

Operant Conditioning. **Dollard and Miller (1950)** claimed that babies feel discomfort when they're hungry and so have a desire to get food to **remove the discomfort**. They find that if they cry, their mother will come and feed them — so the discomfort is removed (this is '**negative reinforcement**'). An easy life. The mother is therefore associated with food and the baby will want to be close to her. This produces 'attachment behaviour' (distress when separated from the mother, etc.).

Learning Theory Has Strengths and Weaknesses

Some comments on the learning theory of attachment include:

- The learning theory of attachment has lots of **support** from **scientific research**.
- But it is **reductionist** — it tries to explain complex attachment using simple stimulus-response processes.
- Lots of the evidence for learning theory uses **animal research**, so the findings aren't always **generalisable**.
- Schaffer and Emerson's (1964) findings don't fully support learning theory. In their study, half of the infants didn't have their mother as the primary attachment.
- There are **other theories** of attachment which also have support, such as Bowlby's theory (see below).

John Bowlby's Monotropic Theory of Attachment is an Evolutionary Theory

Bowlby (1951) argued that something like imprinting (p.28) occurs in humans.
He went on to develop several main claims:

1) Attachment Can Be Explained by Evolution

We have **evolved** a **biological need** to attach to our main caregiver.
This biological need has developed through **natural selection** to ensure the **survival** of the child to maturity.

2) We Create One Special Attachment

Bowlby's idea of **monotropy** is that we form one **main attachment** — usually to our biological mother.
Forming this attachment has **survival value**, as staying close to the mother ensures food and protection.
A strong attachment provides a '**safe base**', giving us confidence to explore our environment.

3) We Create an Internal Working Model of Attachment

Bowlby's theory also says that forming an infant attachment gives us a '**template**' for all future relationships — we learn to trust and care for others. This forms an **internal working model** for all later attachments.

The model is a '**working**' model because it can **change** and **develop** over time, depending on how the person's relationships change. See page 38 to see how it helps to explain the formation of adult relationships.

The primary caregiver provides the foundations for the child's future relationships.
This is called the **continuity hypothesis**.

Explanations of Attachment

4) There is a Critical Period for Attachment

The first three years of life are the **critical period** for attachment to develop — otherwise it might never do so.

If the attachment doesn't develop (e.g. because of separation or death), or if it's broken, it might seriously damage the child's social and emotional development (see pages 34-37).

Bowlby's **'maternal deprivation hypothesis'** (p.34) assumes if the relationship between the primary caregiver (often mother) and infant is disrupted or stopped during the critical period, there are long-term consequences.

It was critical that Jimmy bonded with Terrence from the moment they first met.

Comments on Bowlby's Theory

1) There is some **evidence** for his claims. **Harlow's** study supports the idea that we have evolved a need to attach. It also suggests that social and emotional development might be damaged if an attachment isn't formed. See page 38 for another study that supports Bowlby's theory.

2) **Schaffer and Emerson (1964)** provided evidence against Bowlby's claims about monotropy. They found that, rather than one main attachment, many children form **multiple attachments**, and may not attach to their mother (see page 26).

3) **Harlow's** study of monkeys raised in isolation (p.28) also goes against the idea of **monotropy**. Other monkeys who didn't have a mother, but who grew up together, didn't show signs of social and emotional disturbance in later life. They didn't have a primary caregiver, but seemed to attach to each other instead.

4) There is **mixed evidence** for claims of a **critical period** for attachments to develop (see above, page 28 and page 38).

5) The effect of attachment not developing, or being broken, may not be as bad as Bowlby claimed (see p.35).

6) Bowlby's report in the 1950s led to an **increase** in **'stay at home'** mothering. This had a subsequent **impact on the economy** as fewer women were going to work.

Practice Questions

Q1 How can classical conditioning be used to explain attachment?

Q2 What is 'monotropy'?

Q3 What is Bowlby's internal working model?

Q4 How long does Bowlby's critical period for attachment last for?

Exam Questions

Q1 Read the report, then answer the question that follows.

> Amy's mother rejected her from an early age and she was brought up by various family members. Amy is now six, and struggles to maintain her own friendships or develop any attachments with her peers.

Suggest how Bowlby's internal working model of attachment might explain Amy's current relationships. [4 marks]

Q2 Evaluate Bowlby's theory of attachment. [4 marks]

Q3 Outline the learning theory of attachment. [6 marks]

I'm really quite attached to that giant piece of lemon drizzle cake...

There's more than one explanation of attachment, but don't get overwhelmed. Just think of the two on these pages as two main perspectives. Learning theory suggests our attachments are created from our experiences, whereas Bowlby's theory suggests there is some biological and natural drive causing us to develop attachments. Exciting stuff...

Types of Attachment

If you enjoyed the last two pages, then you're gonna love these ones. As you know, an 'attachment' is a strong, emotional bond between two people. Psychologists are interested in how our first attachments form and what influences them.

Attachments Can Be **Secure** or **Insecure**

Secure Attachments

In a secure attachment, there's a **strong bond** between the child and its caregiver. If they're separated, the infant becomes **distressed**. However, when they're reunited, the child is **easily comforted** by the caregiver. The majority of attachments are of this type. Secure attachments are associated with a healthy cognitive and emotional development.

This might also be called 'Type B'.

Insecure Attachments

Attachments can also be insecure. Here, the bond between child and caregiver is **weaker**. Ainsworth et al came up with **two types** of insecure attachment:

Insecure-avoidant

If they're separated from their caregiver, the child **doesn't** become particularly distressed, and can usually be comforted by a **stranger**. This type of insecure attachment is shown by children who generally **avoid** social interaction and intimacy with others.

This is also known as 'anxious-avoidant' or 'Type A'.

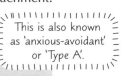

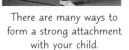

There are many ways to form a strong attachment with your child.

Insecure-resistant

The child is often **uneasy** around their caregiver, but becomes **upset** if they're separated. Comfort can't be given by strangers, and it's also often **resisted** from the caregiver. Children who show this style of attachment both **accept** and **reject** social interaction and intimacy.

This is also known as 'anxious-resistant' or 'Type C'.

An Infant's **Reaction** in a **Strange Situation** Shows if It's **Securely** Attached

Ainsworth came up with the concept of the **strange situation**. She used it to assess how children react under conditions of **stress** (by separation from the caregiver and the presence of a stranger) and also to **new situations**.

	Ainsworth et al (1978) — The strange situation
Method:	In a **controlled observation**, 12-18 month old infants were left in a room with their mother. Eight different scenarios occurred, including being approached by a stranger, the infant being left alone, and the mother returning. The infant's reactions were constantly observed.
Results:	About 15% of infants were **'insecure-avoidant' (type A)** — they ignored their mother and didn't mind if she left. A stranger could comfort them. About 70% were **'securely attached' (type B)** — they were content with their mother, upset when she left, and happy when she returned. They also avoided strangers. About 15% were **'insecure-resistant' (type C)** — they were uneasy around their mother and upset if she left. They resisted strangers and were also hard to comfort when their mother returned.
Conclusion:	Infants showing different reactions to their carers have different types of attachment.
Evaluation:	The research method used allowed control of the variables, making the results reliable. However, the laboratory-type situation made the study artificial, **reducing** the ecological validity. The parents may have changed their behaviour, as they knew that they were being observed. This could have had an effect on the children's behaviour. Also, the new situation in the experiment may have had an effect on the children's behaviour — the study might not accurately represent their behaviour in real life. Another problem is that the mother may not have been the child's **main attachment figure**.

Types of Attachment

Similar Studies Have Taken Place in *Different Cultures*

Ainsworth et al's (1978) findings have been shown many times in the **USA**, but it wasn't then known whether they could be applied to other **cultures**. **Cross-cultural studies** have since taken place:

Van Ijzendoorn and Kroonenberg (1988) — Cross-cultural studies

Method:	Van Ijzendoorn and Kroonenberg carried out a meta-analysis of 32 studies of 'the strange situation' in different countries (e.g. Japan, Britain, Sweden, etc.). They were analysed to find any overall patterns.
Results:	The percentages of children classified as secure or insecure were **similar** across the countries tested — there were more differences within the actual countries than between them. Secure attachments were the most common type of attachment in the countries studied. Some differences were found in the distribution of insecure attachments. In Western cultures, the dominant type of insecure attachment was **avoidant**, with the highest proportion of insecure-avoidant children coming from Germany. However, in non-Western cultures, the dominant type of insecure attachment was **resistant**. Here, Japan had the highest proportion of insecure-resistant children.
Conclusion:	There are cross-cultural similarities in raising children, with common reactions to the 'strange situation'.
Evaluation:	Children are brought up in different ways in different cultures. This might result in different types of attachment in different cultures. Because of this, the 'strange situation' might not be a suitable method for studying cross-cultural attachment. Using a **different type** of study may have revealed different patterns or types of attachment in different cultures. Also, the study assumes that different **countries** are the same thing as different **cultures**. One problem with the research method is that meta-analyses can **hide** individual results that show an unusual trend.

There are Important *Findings* from Strange Situation Research

1) **Some cultural differences are found. Grossman et al (1985)** claimed that more 'avoidant' infants may be found in Germany because of the value Germans put on independence — so 'avoidance' is seen as good.

2) **The causes of different attachment types are debatable.**
The causes may be the sensitivity of their carers and/or their inborn temperament.

3) **The strange situation experiment doesn't show a characteristic of the child.** The experiment only shows the child's relationship with a specific person, so they might react differently with different carers, or later in life.

4) **Attachment type may influence later behaviours.** Securely attached children may be more confident in school and form strong, trusting adult relationships (p.38). 'Avoidant' children may have behaviour problems in school and find it hard to form close, trusting adult relationships. 'Resistant' children may be insecure and attention-seeking in school and, as adults, their strong feelings of dependency may be stressful for partners.

Practice Questions

Q1 What is a secure attachment?
Q2 What are the two types of insecure attachment?
Q3 Who came up with the 'strange situation'?
Q4 What have cross-cultural studies shown about attachments?

Exam Questions

Q1 a) Outline and evaluate Ainsworth et al's (1978) 'strange situation' study. [8 marks]

b) Explain **two** disadvantages of using the 'strange situation' in a study of attachment. [4 marks]

Try to get all these ideas firmly attached to the inside of your head...

Next time you're in trouble at school types your parents are called in to 'discuss your behaviour', try sobbing gently under your breath, 'I think it's all my insecure-resistant attachment formation — it's left me insecure and needy of attention'. It's a desperate attempt, but it might just make your parents feel bad enough to let you off.

Disruption of Attachment

The attachments we form are pretty important — there can be serious consequences if they're broken...

Attachment Can Be Disrupted by **Separation** or **Deprivation**

Separation is where a child is away from a **caregiver** they're attached to (such as their mother). The term's used when it's a **relatively short** time, just hours or days — not a longer or permanent separation.

Deprivation describes the loss of something that is **wanted or needed**. So, 'maternal deprivation' is the loss of the mother (or other attachment figure). A more **long-term** or even **permanent** loss is implied.

*John Bowlby (1953) Studied Longer-Term **Maternal Deprivation***

John Bowlby argued that long-term **deprivation** from an attachment figure could be harmful. He produced his **maternal deprivation hypothesis**:

1) Deprivation from the main carer during the **critical period** (the first 3 years) will have harmful effects on a child's emotional, social, intellectual and even physical development. Not so good.

2) Long-term effects of deprivation may include **separation anxiety** (the fear of another separation from the carer). This may lead to problem behaviour, e.g. being very clingy, and avoiding going to school. Future relationships may be affected by this emotional insecurity. Bowlby's research showed evidence for this.

Bowlby (1944) — The 44 juvenile thieves

Method:	**Case studies** were completed on the backgrounds of 44 adolescents who had been referred to the clinic where Bowlby worked because they'd been stealing. There was a **control group** of 44 'emotionally disturbed' adolescents who didn't steal.
Results:	17 of the thieves had experienced frequent separations from their mothers before the age of two, compared with 2 in the control group. 14 of the thieves were diagnosed as 'affectionless psychopaths' (they didn't care about how their actions affected others). 12 of these 14 had experienced separation from their mothers.
Conclusion:	Deprivation of the child from its main carer early in life can have very **harmful long-term consequences**.
Evaluation:	The results indicate a link between deprivation and criminal behaviour. However, it can't be said that one **causes** the other. There may be **other factors** (e.g. poverty) that caused the criminal behaviour. Although case studies provide a lot of **detailed information**, the study relied on **retrospective data**, which may be unreliable.

*Evidence of **Maternal Deprivation** from **Separation** Studies*

Studies which have investigated the effects of short-term separation can also support the idea of Bowlby's **maternal deprivation hypothesis**:

Robertson and Robertson (1968) — A separation study

Method:	In a naturalistic observation, several children who experienced short separations from their carers were observed and filmed. For example, a boy called John aged around 18 months stayed in a residential nursery for nine days while his mother had another baby.
Results:	For the first day or two, John **protested** at being separated from his mother. He then started trying to get attention from the nurses, but they were busy with other children so he gave up trying. After another few days, he began to show signs of **detachment** — he was more active and content than he had been previously at the nursery. But, when his mother came to collect him, he was reluctant to be affectionate.
Conclusion:	The short-term separation had very **bad effects** on John, including possible **permanent damage** to his attachment with his mother.
Evaluation:	John's reaction might not have been due to separation — it could have been down to his new environment or the fact that he was getting much less attention than he was used to. There will have been little control of **variables**, and it would be difficult to replicate each **individual situation**. However, as the study took place in a natural setting, the results will have **ecological validity** but will be less **reliable**.

Disruption of Attachment

Bowlby's *Maternal Deprivation Hypothesis* has *Strengths* and *Weaknesses*

Strengths:
Other evidence **supports** Bowlby's claims. **Goldfarb (1943)** found that orphanage children who were socially and maternally deprived were later less intellectually and socially developed.

Weaknesses:
The **evidence** can be criticised. Bowlby linked the thieves' behaviour to maternal deprivation, but **other things were not considered**, e.g. whether the poverty they grew up in led them to steal. The children in Goldfarb's study may have been most harmed by the **social deprivation** in the orphanage rather than the maternal deprivation.

The *Effects* of *Disruption of Attachment* Can be *Reversed*

One of Bowlby's **assumptions** of his maternal deprivation hypothesis was that the consequences were **not** reversible. However, further research has shown that even when deprivation has harmful effects, these may be reversed with appropriate, **good-quality care**.

Skeels and Dye (1939) found that children who had been socially deprived (in an orphanage) during their first two years of life quickly **improved** their **IQ scores** if they were transferred to a school where they got one-to-one care.

Koluchova (1976) — The Case of the Czech Twin Boys

This is the case of **twin boys** whose mother died soon after they were born. Their father remarried and their stepmother treated them very cruelly. They were often kept locked in a cellar, had no toys and were often beaten.

They were found when they were seven with rickets (a bone development disease caused by a lack of vitamin D), and **very little social or intellectual development**.

They were later adopted and made **much progress**. By adulthood they had above average intelligence and had normal social relationships.

Luckily for Hilda and Mary, the only setback to a disrupted attachment in childhood was the lack of hair straighteners.

Practice Questions

Q1 What does Bowlby's maternal deprivation hypothesis propose?
Q2 Give one weakness of Bowlby's maternal deprivation hypothesis.
Q3 Give one example of when the effects of a disruption of attachment have been reversed.

Exam Questions

Q1 Outline one study that supports Bowlby's theory of maternal deprivation. [4 marks]

Q2 Outline and evaluate Bowlby's theory of maternal deprivation. [12 marks]

So if you're left alone for a while at age 2, you may become a bank robber...

Sounds like a pretty poor excuse to me, but there you go. This is all certainly interesting stuff. Just make sure you learn it all. Including all the studies. If you know the details, you can pick up extra marks in the exam.

Effects of Institutionalisation

It's really easy to get privation and deprivation confused. But it's a good idea to make sure you know the difference between the two — institutionalisation often refers to privation rather than deprivation.

There's a **Difference** Between **Privation** and **Deprivation**

Rutter criticised Bowlby's **maternal deprivation hypothesis**, saying that Bowlby was confused with the term 'deprivation'. He used it to refer to several things — separation from the mother, loss of the mother, and failure to develop an attachment with the mother. These things are now split into deprivation and privation.

> **Privation** is where a child has **never** had an attachment to its mother or caregiver.
>
> **Deprivation** is where an attachment was once formed but is now **broken**.

In reality, it is very **difficult** to distinguish between them.

When Sophie was deprived of her blanket things got ugly.

A **Case Study** of **Privation**

Rutter (1981) claimed that the effects of **maternal privation** are more likely to be **serious** than the effects of **maternal deprivation**. Evidence for this comes from **case studies** of children who have suffered through difficult conditions or cruel treatment. A nasty case study coming up...

> **Curtiss (1977) — The Case of Genie**
>
> This reported the case of a girl who suffered **extreme cruelty** from her parents, and never formed any attachments. Her father kept her strapped to a high chair with a potty in the seat for most of her childhood. She was beaten if she made any sounds, and didn't have the chance to play with toys or with other children.
>
> She was finally discovered when she was 13 years old. She was **physically underdeveloped** and could only speak with **animal-like sounds**. After a lot of help she later learned some language, but her **social and intellectual skills never seemed to fully develop**.

Romanian **Orphan** Studies

The fall of the communist regime in Romania during the early 1990s allowed the world to see the vast overcrowding in their orphanages. The orphans were fed, clothed and looked after, but they lacked any form of **sensitive care** or any opportunity to form an **emotional attachment**.

Since then, various studies of Romanian orphans have enabled psychologists to look directly at the impacts of **privation**.

Studies of children raised in **institutions** (e.g. orphanages) may provide **more reliable data** than case studies, as sample sizes are so much bigger.

	Rutter et al (2007) — A longitudinal study of Romanian orphans
Method:	111 Romanian orphans who were adopted by British families were compared with a group of 52 UK adoptees and followed over a prolonged period. Some of the orphans were adopted before they were 6 months old and some were older than 6 months. Each child was assessed at ages 4, 6 and 11.
Results:	The children who were **younger** than 6 months when they were adopted had the same level of emotional development as other UK children who were adopted at the same age. However, the Romanian orphans who were **older** than 6 months at adoption showed signs of insecure attachments and social problems. The **UK children** who were older than 6 months at adoption didn't show the same problems.
Conclusion:	The effects of privation can be **reversed** if an attachment starts to form **before** the age of 6 months. **Long-term** effects are more **permanent** if attachment doesn't start to occur within 6 months. Maternal deprivation on its own doesn't cause permanent effects because the UK adopted children had been separated but didn't show any problems.
Evaluation:	The results with the older children may be due to a lack of any stimulation in the orphanage. As a **longitudinal study**, Rutter was able to investigate the children over a long period of time, meaning the results provide a better insight into the long-term effects of privation. However, they collected mainly **qualitative** data which, although detailed, is more difficult to create **generalised laws** or **theories** from.

Effects of Institutionalisation

Hodges and Tizard (1989) Studied Early Institutional Care

Rutter et al's research into institutionalisation built upon the research by **Hodges and Tizard (1989)**.

	Hodges and Tizard (1989) — Children raised in institutions.
Method:	This was a **longitudinal** (long-term) study of 65 children who had been placed in a residential nursery before they were four months old. They hadn't had the opportunity to form close attachments with any of their caregivers. By the age of four, some of the children had returned to their birth mothers, some had been adopted, and some had stayed in the nursery.
Results:	At 16 years old, the **adopted** group had **strong** family relationships, although compared to a control group of children from a 'normal' home environment, they had weaker peer relationships. Those who stayed in the **nursery** or who returned to their **mothers** showed **poorer** relationships with family and peers than those who were adopted.
Conclusion:	Children can **recover** from early maternal privation if they are in a good **quality**, **loving** environment, although their social development may not be as good as children who have never suffered privation.
Evaluation:	This was a **natural experiment**, so it had **high ecological validity**. However, the sample was quite **small** and more than 20 of the children couldn't be found at the end of the study, so it's hard to **generalise** the results. Because lots of institutionalised children are unfortunately often **underfed** and **malnourished**, with a lack of stimulation, it could be these factors that influence their behaviour, rather than the lack of attachment itself.

Studies Have Suggested Long-Term Effects of Institutionalisation...

Bowlby's study of the **44 juvenile thieves**, Rutter et al's (2007) study on **Romanian orphans** and others on institutionalisation and hospitalisation, have suggested that long-term effects of disrupted attachments can include:

1) **Affectionless psychopathy** (as seen in the 44 juvenile thieves study).

2) **Anaclitic depression** — involving appetite loss, sleeplessness and impaired social and intellectual development.

3) **Deprivation dwarfism** — infants are physically underdeveloped due to emotional deprivation.

4) **Delinquency** — minor crimes committed by youths.

5) **Reduced intelligence** — infants don't develop intellectually as fast as their peers.

Practice Questions

Q1 What is the difference between privation and deprivation?

Q2 What research method did Rutter et al (2007) use in their Romanian orphan study?

Q3 Outline the strengths and weaknesses of Hodges and Tizard's (1989) study.

Exam Questions

Q1 Discuss, with reference to research, the effects of institutionalisation on young children. [8 marks]

Q2 Read the item below, then answer the question that follows.

> Meryl was a troubled teenager. Her school report continued to outline her struggle to form social relationships with her peers, her failing results and her turn to petty crime. Meryl had been adopted from an orphanage at the age of 6.

With reference to Meryl's behaviour, outline **two** effects of institutionalisation. [4 marks]

Developmental problems — enough to make you develop mental problems...

There are some pretty grisly studies on these pages. It may not be the nicest of topics, but it is interesting to see how these theories of privation and deprivation fit within developmental psychology. My advice would be to get the theories and studies in your head quickly and move on to the next bit. Maybe make yourself a hot chocolate too...

Early Attachment and Later Relationships

It kind of makes sense that our early attachments and relationships will influence the relationships we might have as adults. But psychologists like to study these things in depth anyway. So take a look at these pages...

The Internal Working Model Helps Explain Adult Relationships

Bowlby's **internal working model** (page 30) looked at how our childhood attachments influence adult relationships.

> **Examples**
>
> - If a child has a **secure attachment** to a **sensitive** caregiver, they are likely to see themselves as **worthy** of being loved. They are then likely to form future **secure relationships**.
> - If a child has an **insecure attachment** with a caregiver who rejects them, they are likely to see themselves as **unworthy** of being loved. They are then likely to form future **insecure relationships**.

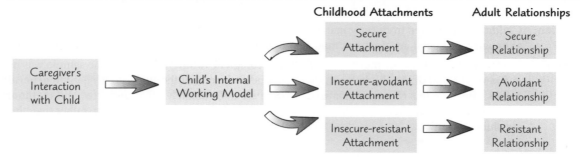

Hazan and Shaver (1987) developed a study to explore how early attachment can predict adult relationships.

Hazan and Shaver (1987) — The influence of early attachments

Method:	Hazan and Shaver conducted a 'love quiz' in a local newspaper. The quiz had two parts. The first part assessed the attachment type of each person with their parents. The second part involved questions asking about their current beliefs about romantic love.
Results:	The first 620 responses were analysed. They found that there was a correlation between the type of childhood attachment and people's later views on romantic love. Secure children were more likely to have happy and trustworthy relationships. Insecure-avoidant children ended up fearing intimacy and insecure-resistant children were more likely to be worried that they weren't loved in their relationships.
Conclusion:	Hazan and Shaver concluded that their findings provided **support** for Bowlby's **internal working model** — that early attachments **do** influence adult relationships.
Evaluation:	The quiz relied on people thinking back to their childhood, which isn't always accurate. Additionally, the study used a **volunteer sample**, so a certain type of person might be more likely to respond. Also, people may have answered untruthfully to show themselves in a better light. However, they did repeat the study in 2003, and found similar results.

The Adult Attachment Interview Explored the Role of Early Attachments

Psychologists developed a way to try to scientifically assess the relationship between early childhood attachments and later adult attachments. They came up with the **adult attachment interview**.

It's based on the idea that it doesn't really matter exactly **what** the childhood attachment was — it's **how** it was remembered. This again supports the **internal working model**.

Main et al (1985) — The Adult Attachment Interview

This **semi-structured interview** involves a series of questions about childhood attachment relationships, and how these were seen to influence later relationships. The interviewee is asked to give **five adjectives** explaining their relationship with each of their parents. They're then asked to explain why they chose each adjective. Other questions are then asked about times they got upset, if they ever felt rejected, and how they believe their early experiences influenced their adult attachments. The results are then **classified** by trained coders into a category — **secure, dismissing, preoccupied** or **unresolved/disorganised**.

Main et al (1985) went on to show that the categories of adult relationships could be predicted from people's recall of their childhood attachments.

Early Attachment and Later Relationships

Research Suggests Two **Long-Term Effects** of **Privation**

The **Cycle of Privation**

Some studies suggest that children who experience **privation** go on to have difficulties caring for their own children:

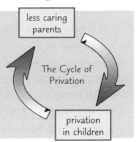

Quinton et al (1984) compared 50 women who had experienced institutional care as children with 50 women who hadn't. They found that the women who had been raised in institutions were more likely to have parenting difficulties later in life. This suggests that there is a **cycle of privation** — children who have experienced privation later go on to become less caring parents. Therefore, their children are deprived of a strong maternal attachment and may then be less caring to their children, and so on.

Reactive Attachment Disorder — Parker and Forrest (1993)

Parker and Forrest (1993) outlined this rare but serious condition, which occurs in children who have been **permanently damaged** by early experiences such as **privation** of attachment. Symptoms include:

1) an inability to give or receive affection
2) dishonesty
3) poor social relationships
4) involvement in crime

But It's Not All **Bad...**

Freud and Dann (1951) showed that privation might not necessarily lead to detrimental outcomes.

Freud and Dann (1951) studied six children who were rescued after WWII. They had been orphaned during the war at a few months old, and raised within a deportation camp. Although they were looked after by the Jewish people 'passing through' to the concentration camps, the children didn't have time to form any adult attachments, instead forming bonds amongst themselves. When the war ended, the children were adopted by British families and have since shown few signs of a troubled upbringing, having a **normal level of intelligence** and maintaining **normal relationships**.

Practice Questions

Q1 Give an example of a study which supports Bowlby's internal working model.
Q2 What useful assessment tool did Main et al (1985) develop?
Q3 What is the 'cycle of privation'?
Q4 Describe Freud and Dann's (1951) case study of the German orphans.

Exam Question

Q1 Read the item below, then answer the question that follows.

> As an infant, Norman was often uneasy around his mother, but when he was dropped off at school, he would cry and wail all day. When Norman grew up and went to university, he was fearful of forming any romantic relationships and any time he did get feelings for anyone, he became anxious and overwhelmed.

Use Bowlby's internal working model to explain Norman's behaviour towards others. [4 marks]

My mum is a bit bonkers — what does that mean I'll be like as a parent...?

As with everything in psychology, there are studies that support and refute the main theories. So, although some studies say that early attachments do affect later relationships, there are also those that don't. Gah... nothing is simple these days. But — on a side note, once you've learnt these pages, you're done with attachment. For now.

The Origins of Psychology

Once upon a time (around 1879), there was a man called Wilhelm who lived in a pleasant German city. He decided to set up a psychology lab. And from there, modern psychology as we know it was born...

Psychology is a Science with **Lots of Theories** and **Few Facts**

Psychology is "**the scientific study of the mind and behaviour**".
This basically means that psychologists look at what people and animals do, why they do it, and how they feel.

A lot of psychology sounds like **common sense**, but it's a science, so everything's got to be investigated. You've got to come up with a **theory** about something and then **scientifically test** it.

It's difficult to prove things in psychology, so there are loads of disagreements and a lot of theories that sound rubbish. But you can't just say they're rubbish in your exam — that'd be too easy. No, you've got to use other theories and experiments to support your answer.

The different schools of thought are called **approaches**. Each approach has its own explanation for why we do what we do. You'll be looking at the **behavioural**, **cognitive** and **biological** approaches. There are others too, but you don't need to worry about them just yet.

Wundt was the *Father* of Experimental Psychology

> Structuralism breaks down human thoughts and experiences into basic components.

Wilhelm Wundt (1832 – 1920)

In 1879, **Wilhelm Wundt** opened an **Institute for Experimental Psychology** in Germany. He separated psychology from philosophy and focused on studying the mind in a much more structured and scientific way. Using a **structuralist** and **reductionist** (see below) approach, Wundt used methods such as **introspection** to try to uncover what people were thinking and experiencing.

Introspection *Involves Looking into Your Mind*

Introspection is a psychological method which involves analysing your own thoughts and feelings internally.

In the 1800s, there were no brain scans or computers to enable people to explore the inside workings of the brain. So, as a way to investigate people's consciousness, Wundt used **introspection** to study **sensation** and **perception**. Participants were asked to describe their experiences when presented with a set of stimuli, and often their reaction times were recorded.

> Introspection allowed Wundt to analyse the quality of the sensations people experienced.

Problems with Introspection
- It doesn't explain **how** the mind works. It relies on people describing their thoughts and feelings, which usually isn't **objective**.
- It doesn't provide data that can be used **reliably**. Because people are reporting on their experiences, their accounts can't be confirmed.

Even though Wundt's method of introspection wasn't that objective, his experimental approach to psychology did influence other areas of the subject. These include the beginnings of the **behavioural**, **cognitive** and **biological** approaches.

Shaun's experience of wearing a onesie was slightly different to others'.

Wundt Believed in **Reductionism**

Reductionism is the idea that things can be reduced to simple cause-and-effect processes. Wundt came from a biological background, and so he believed that the underlying structure of human experience could be broken down into smaller, **measurable** parts. He used introspection to measure these parts.

The Origins of Psychology

But is Psychology a *Science*?

Wundt's founding of experimental psychology kicked psychology into the scientific world. It could now be taken much more seriously. But there is still a lot of **controversy** around the idea that it is a **true science**.

There are several features that make something a science:

1) **Objectivity** — scientific observations should be recorded without bias and not influenced by any other factors, or any other people.

2) **Control** — scientific observations should take place under controlled conditions.

3) **Predictability** — scientists should be able to use the results and knowledge gained from experiments to predict future behaviour.

4) **Hypothesis testing** — theories generate predictions (hypotheses) which can be tested to either strengthen the support for the theory, or else disprove it.

5) **Replication** — each experiment should be able to be replicated exactly so people can have confidence in the results.

See page 78 for more on hypotheses.

There are Arguments *For* and *Against* Psychology as a Science

The debate around whether psychology can be called a science continues to the present day.

Arguments For:

- **Allport (1947)** said psychology has the same aims as science — to **predict**, **understand** and **control**.
- Behaviourist, cognitive and biological approaches to psychology all use **scientific procedures** to investigate theories. They are usually controlled and unbiased.

Arguments Against:

- There are other approaches in psychology which don't use objective methods to study behaviour. They use **unreliable** methods — e.g. interview techniques which can be **biased** and interpreted differently by different researchers.
- It's very hard to get a **representative** sample of the population for a study, so findings can't reliably be **generalised**.
- Psychological experiments are also open to **extraneous variables**, such as **demand characteristics** (when participants try to guess the aim of the study), which can be hard to control.

Practice Questions

Q1 What role did Wilhelm Wundt play in the development of psychology?

Q2 What is 'introspection'?

Q3 What is 'reductionism'?

Q4 Describe five features of a science.

Exam Questions

Q1 Outline how psychology has emerged as a science. [6 marks]

Q2 Is psychology a science? Discuss this statement using what you know about the origins of psychology. [8 marks]

Q3 What did Wundt study using introspection?
    A Brain waves   **B** Memory   **C** Sensation   **D** Attachment [1 mark]

Wundt's da Daddy...

It all started long ago... well, actually not really that long ago. Psychology is a relatively new discipline, but it has a lot going for it. When Wundt first started his Institute for Experimental Psychology, little did he know how we'd all be revising away for our Psychology exams over 100 years later. He must be so proud.

Behaviourism — Classical and Operant Conditioning

There are lots of different approaches to the study of psychology, including the behaviourist, cognitive and biological approaches. First things first then — introducing the behaviourist approach...

Behaviourism is Also Known as 'Learning Theory'

1) Behaviourism ('**Learning Theory**') started in America in the early 1900s, mainly through the ideas of **John Watson**.

2) Watson felt that earlier psychological research wasn't as scientific as it should be.

3) For example, Wilhelm Wundt tried to study consciousness using **introspection**. This involves analysing your own experiences. However, there's no way of finding out whether what a person said is true or not, so introspection can never be properly scientific.

4) Watson came up with some assumptions on which to base a **scientific** approach to psychology.

There are **Three** Main **Assumptions** of Behaviourism

Remember — this is theory, not fact.

1) **Nearly all behaviour is learnt.**
   The only exceptions are a few inborn **reflexes** (e.g. blinking when we get dirt in our eyes) and a few inborn **instincts** (e.g. instinctively running when in some types of danger).

   However, evidence now shows that **genetics** can influence psychological features, e.g. genetics may contribute to the development of schizophrenia. Behaviourism still claims, though, that learning, and not genetics, is the cause of the **majority** of behaviours, even if some vague genetic causes can be found.

2) **Animals and humans learn in the same ways.**
   Humans can do much more complex things than other animals, but the **principles** by which we learn are the **same**. So, we learn to drive a car through the same principles as a cat learns to use a cat-flap. This is based on the idea that we can form **stimulus-response associations** between stimuli and our actions. However, although we may both use conditioning, humans can be said to use other forms of learning as well, such as **social learning** (see pages 46-47).

3) **The 'mind' is irrelevant.**
   We can't directly observe and measure a person's thinking. So we can only obtain **measurable data** by studying behaviour.

   However, although **cognitive abilities** cannot be directly, scientifically measured, they may give a more complete explanation of behaviour — as shown by **social learning theory** (see pages 46-47).

'All learnt through stimulus-response associations.' Pretty impressive, but it does beg the question 'why?'

Behaviourists Use Their **Assumptions** to Design **Research Methods**

The research methods used by behaviourists follow directly from their **assumptions**, as follows:

1 — Nearly all behaviour is learnt.
So, understanding the principles of **learning** is the main research goal.

2 — Animals and humans learn in the same ways.
Animals can be used as research subjects because what is true for them should also be true for humans. Using animals has **practical advantages**, e.g. they are easy to keep, in many circumstances they don't know they are being studied and so behave 'naturally', and procedures can be used with them which would be illegal with humans (e.g. administering shocks as punishment to see the effect on learning).

3 — The 'mind' is irrelevant.
Behaviourists only observe **quantifiable behaviour** — e.g. how many times a lever is pressed, or how long it takes to solve a puzzle. Typical research therefore involves **laboratory experiments** on animals, to see how they learn.

Behaviourism — Classical and Operant Conditioning

Behaviourists Proposed **Two Types** of Conditioning:

1) *Classical Conditioning*

In early 1900s Russia, **Ivan Pavlov** was studying how dogs' salivation helps them to digest food, when he noticed that they would sometimes salivate **before** they got food. Instead of just thinking they were hungry, he realised they had **associated** food with another stimulus, such as the sound of the door opening. Pavlov started to experiment...

1) Whenever Pavlov gave his dogs some food, he would also ring a bell. After repeating this procedure several times, Pavlov then tried ringing the bell without giving the dogs any food. The bell alone caused salivation.

2) When dogs see food, they salivate. This is an automatic, unlearned response — a reflex. The food is an **unconditioned stimulus (UCS)** and salivation is an **unconditioned response (UCR)**.

3) The bell had become a **conditioned stimulus (CS)**, and salivation had become a **conditioned response (CR)**.

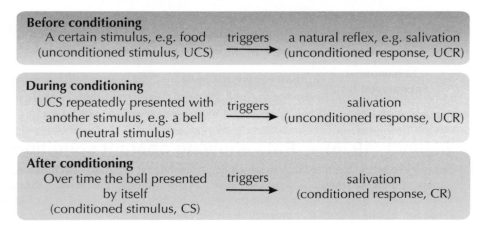

He later made the dogs associate food with lights and other abstract stimuli.
This process of learning can be applied to human development:

Having its needs dealt with and gaining comfort naturally makes a baby happy. It hasn't **learnt** to be happy. It's an **inborn reflex**.

So, comfort is an **unconditioned stimulus (UCS)** that produces happiness — an **unconditioned response (UCR)**.

The baby's mother will talk to it while she feeds it and changes its nappy, etc. So, the baby hears its mother's voice every time it's made comfortable and happy.

The sound of its mother's voice is paired with having needs met and being comfortable (**UCS**), so the mother's voice becomes a **conditioned stimulus (CS)**.

Eventually the sound of the mother's voice alone will make the baby feel happy, even when it isn't paired with having its needs met. The **CS** (voice) now causes a **conditioned response (CR)** — the baby has **learnt** to be pleased at the sound of its mother's voice.

There are Several **Principles** of Classical Conditioning

- **Generalisation** — when stimuli similar to the original CS (e.g. a bell with a different pitch) produce the CR (e.g. salivating).
- **Discrimination** — when stimuli similar to the original CS don't produce the CR. This can be achieved by withholding the UCS (e.g. food) when the similar stimulus is used.
- **Extinction** — when the CR (e.g. salivating) isn't produced as a result of the CS (e.g. bell). This happens when the CS is repeatedly presented without the UCS (e.g. food) following it.
- **Spontaneous recovery** — when a previously extinct CR is produced in response to the CS. This happens when the CS is presented again after a period of time during which it's not been used.
- **Higher order conditioning** — when a new CS (e.g. a light) produces the CR because the animal associates it with the original CS. This can be achieved by consistently presenting the new CS before the original CS.

Behaviourism — Classical and Operant Conditioning

2) Operant Conditioning

Classical conditioning only applies to reflexive responses. **B.F. Skinner** studied how animals can learn from the **consequences of their actions**. Consequences can be classified as follows:

1) **Positive reinforcement**. This is when something 'desirable' is obtained in response to doing something. E.g. giving a chocolate bar to a well-behaved child to encourage future good behaviour.

2) **Negative reinforcement**. This is when something 'undesirable' (the negative reinforcer) is removed when something happens. E.g. being told by the teacher that you'll have no extra homework if you pass your test.

	Positive **stimulus added**	**Negative** **stimulus added**
Behaviour is **encouraged by...**	*positive reinforcement*	*negative reinforcement*

	Skinner (1938) — Rats showing operant conditioning
Method:	Skinner created a 'Skinner box', in which he placed one rat at a time. Each Skinner box contained a variety of different stimuli — a speaker, lights, a floor which gave an electric shock and a food dispenser which released food when a lever was pressed. A hungry rat was placed in the Skinner box. The time taken for the rats to learn that pressing the lever would release food was recorded.
Results:	Initially, the rat would run around the cage until it accidentally pressed the lever and it was rewarded with food. The more the rat was put back into the box, the quicker they got at learning where the lever was.
Conclusion:	Rats can learn behaviour through operant conditioning. A behaviour such as pressing a lever can be positively reinforced by receiving food.
Evaluation:	Skinner's experiment has been hugely influential in promoting the idea of behavioural psychology. However, his experiment did use animals, which means the results might not be generalisable to humans. His sample size was also small, reducing the reliability of his results.

Skinner carried out other variations of this study to test **negative reinforcement**.
E.g. he showed that a rat could learn to **prevent** an electric shock by pressing the lever when a light came on.

Conditioning Has **Strengths** and **Weaknesses**

- There's a lot of evidence to show that animals and humans can learn by conditioning, but conditioning can't explain all human behaviour. We also learn by observation, as shown by **social learning theory** (p.46-47).

- Most research into conditioning has involved animals. This means generalising to humans is difficult. More research into human conditioning would be useful.

- Different species have different capacities for learning by conditioning. Some may also learn by simple observation, with no reinforcement involved.

- Genetics seem to influence and limit what different species can learn by conditioning.

- Lots of experiments into learning in animals may be seen as unethical. Nowadays, researchers have to conduct a cost-benefit analysis of whether it's acceptable to use animals, and they must ensure that any animals are well looked after.

Behaviourism — Classical and Operant Conditioning

Behaviourist Research Has Provided Great *Insights* into Learning

1) Along with Pavlov's research into classical conditioning using dogs, and Skinner's research into operant conditioning using rats, research has been carried out using humans.

2) One experiment which involved humans was Watson and Rayner's experiment on '**Little Albert**':

Watson and Rayner (1920) — Little Albert learned fear

Method: The participant was an 11-month-old boy called 'Little Albert'. He showed no fear of white fluffy objects such as rats or rabbits. The researchers tried to create a conditioned response to these objects.
A white rat was placed in front of Little Albert. As he reached out for it, a metal bar was struck loudly behind his head. This was repeated twice at first, then 5 more times a week later.

Results: When Little Albert was shown a rat, he would start to cry. This also extended to other white fluffy objects, such as a white Santa Claus beard.

Conclusion: A fear response to white fluffy objects had been **conditioned** in Little Albert, showing that abnormal behaviour can be **learned**.

Evaluation: The experiment was very **unethical** — such an experiment couldn't be repeated today. **Not everyone** goes on to develop a fear or phobia after a negative situation, so learning theory can't be the full story. It was a laboratory study, so it **lacks ecological validity** as the situation was artificial. However, the results **support** Pavlov's idea of classical conditioning.

Behaviourists are often criticised for focusing research on animals.
Plenty of research has been done on humans, which has shown things like:

- our **genes** influence our behaviour
- we can **learn in ways other than conditioning**
- **mental, cognitive processes are relevant** to understanding behaviour.

Absolutely nothing to worry about, Mrs Albert — all within the guidelines.

Practice Questions

Q1 What are the three main assumptions of behaviourism?

Q2 Describe the principles of classical conditioning.

Q3 What is 'positive reinforcement'?

Q4 Give an example of negative reinforcement.

Q5 What device did Skinner use to illustrate operant conditioning?

Q6 Outline Watson and Rayner's (1920) method.

Exam Questions

Q1 Describe Pavlov's influence on behavioural psychology. [4 marks]

Q2 Read the item, then answer the question that follows.

> After crying, an infant's dirty nappy is removed.
> The child is likely to cry the next time the nappy needs changing.

What type of reinforcement is shown by the infant? [1 mark]

Learn like a dolphin — lob live fish in the air and catch them in your mouth...

The behaviourists assume that humans and animals learn the same way. Still, I've never met an animal that was scared of Santa. Apart from reindeer, of course — they can't stand him. But that's because there's no pension scheme — once those reindeer can't fly any more, that's it. He sends 'em off to the glue factory and uses their antlers as shoehorns.

Behaviourism — Social Learning Theory

Behavioural psychologists came up with another idea on top of classical and operant conditioning. It's called the social learning theory — and there's a juicy study for you to read all about here. Happy days.

Social Learning Theory (SLT) Expands on Behaviourist Theories

A guy called **Bandura** developed SLT in the 1960s. It agrees with the idea that people can learn by conditioning but also claims that they learn a lot from role models. Some mediational (cognitive) processes are also involved between the stimulus and the response.

People must focus their **attention** on the role model, **perceive** what they do and **remember** it in order to learn how to do it too.

mediational processes

stimulus ➤ response

Behaviour is Learnt Through Different Processes...

SLT proposes that several processes take place for learning to happen:

> **Modelling** involves observing and imitating another person (the **model**). It also requires **identification** with the model — where certain attractive **qualities** and **characteristics** are picked up on. If you identify with the model, you can copy and learn from their behaviour. The model will often be someone who is significant to the observer (e.g. a parent, a celebrity, a peer).
>
> Behaviour can also be learnt through:
>
> - **Reinforcement** — **Positive** and **negative** reinforcement makes the behaviour more likely to happen again in the future.
>
> - **Vicarious Reinforcement** — Seeing others being rewarded for a behaviour influences someone in whether they choose to imitate the behaviour.

... and Mediated Through Cognitive Processes

For effective learning, **mediational processes** need to happen. These are cognitive processes:

1) Attention

To learn a behaviour from others, you have to pay **attention**. Once you notice your role model, you have to give your full attention and **attend** to their behaviour.

2) Retention

Not only do you need to pay attention at the time, but you need to remember what you observed to be able to model it.

'Retention' might also be called 'encoding'.

3) Reproduction

You then judge whether you have the **ability** to reproduce the behaviour. If you think you **can** reproduce the behaviour, you're far more likely to do it. (E.g. if you think you can't juggle with fire, you're unlikely to copy a fire-juggler.)

Jessie modelled her behaviour on 'girl stuck in box'.

4) Motivation

Finally, you **evaluate** the direct or indirect results of imitating the behaviour. If the behaviour results in a good reward, you're more likely to imitate it.

Social Learning Theory is Reductionist

SLT is a **reductionist theory** — it explains things through very basic cause-and-effect mechanisms. For example, it explains all behaviour as a result of **learning** from others, and **ignores** any biological explanations.

Behaviourism — Social Learning Theory

Bandura Studied Imitation of Aggression

Bandura et al (1961) showed successfully how children **imitate** and can be **influenced by** adult role models.

Bandura et al (1961) — Imitation of aggressive models

Method: 36 girls and 36 boys with a mean age of 52 months took part in the study. The study had a **matched participants design** (children were matched on ratings of aggressive behaviour shown at their nursery school) and had **three conditions**. In the first condition, children observed **aggressive adult models** playing with a Bobo doll (an inflatable figure with a weight in the bottom) — e.g. hitting it with a mallet. In the second, children observed **non-aggressive models** playing with other toys and ignoring the Bobo doll. The third condition was a **control condition** in which children had no exposure to the models. The children's behaviour was then observed for 20 minutes in a room containing aggressive toys (e.g. a Bobo doll, a mallet) and non-aggressive toys (e.g. a tea set, crayons).

Results: Children exposed to aggressive models imitated a lot of their aggressive behaviour. Children in the non-aggressive and control conditions showed barely any aggressive behaviour. Aggressive behaviour was slightly higher in the control condition than in the non-aggressive condition.

Conclusion: Aggressive behaviour is learned through **imitation** of others behaving aggressively.

Evaluation: This study provides evidence for **social learning theory**. There was **strict control** of the variables, meaning that the results are likely to be **reliable** and the study can be **replicated**. However, it has **low ecological validity** because the participants weren't in a natural situation. It's also difficult to **generalise** the results because a limited sample was studied — the children were all from the same school. The study encouraged aggression in children — this could be an **ethical problem**.

*Some **Comments** on SLT, Behaviourism and Bandura's Research:*

1) Bandura's study shows that **reinforcement is not needed for learning**. We can learn just by **observing**. However, the reinforcement the model is seen to receive may have an effect — for example, if you see a model punished for an action, you're unlikely to copy it.

2) Bobo dolls are designed for 'aggressive' play — you're **supposed** to hit them. As well as this, the children were shown how to play with the doll, so this study might actually be a test of **obedience** (see page 7) rather than observational learning.

3) Behaviourism and SLT emphasise learning as the cause of behaviour and so are on the **'nurture'** side of the **nature-nurture debate**. This has implications for society. For example, children may imitate aggression from media role models. However, potential **genetic influences** are not taken into account.

4) It can often be **difficult** to conclude that observational learning has taken place. Sometimes, behaviours can be repeated a **long time after** they've been observed.

Practice Questions

Q1 What is 'vicarious reinforcement'?
Q2 What did Bandura et al (1961) find in their study of imitation?
Q3 Give one limitation of social learning theory.

Exam Questions

Q1 Which of these is a not a mediational process proposed by social learning theory?
   A reproduction   **B** reductionism   **C** retention   **D** motivation   [1 mark]

Q2 Outline and evaluate research into social learning theory.   [8 marks]

My dad's just given me a really big slice of chocolate cake for revising...

Hopefully this'll act as some form of vicarious reinforcement to kick-start you into revising these pages. Learning Psychology is all about engaging your mediational processes. You just have to remember what they are first.

The Cognitive Approach

Welcome to the cognitive approach. A fine approach if ever I saw one. A real rollicking riotous romp of an approach —
full of mystery and intrigue, with a few exciting twists and turns along the way. So get comfy on your bedroom floor,
line up your miniature highlighters, and saddle up the revision pony, cos the next stop's Examsville, Arizona...

Cognitive Psychology Looks at How We **Interpret** the World

1) Whilst the behavioural approach studies observable behaviour, the cognitive approach does the opposite —
   it looks at the internal workings of the mind and explains behaviour through **cognitive processes**.
   It is all about **how** we think.

2) Cognitive psychologists try to **explain behaviour** by looking at our **perception**,
   language, **attention** and **memory**.

3) Cognitive psychology uses experimental procedures and methods to test behaviour scientifically.

4) The mind can be compared to a computer, so it is a **reductionist** approach.

5) **Computers** and computer models are often used to explain how we think and behave.
   Humans are treated as **information processors** (computers) and behaviour is
   explained in terms of **information processing** (how computers deal with information).

Cognitive psychology
is sometimes called
the information
processing approach.

6) **Computer** and **theoretical models** are used to **explain** and make **inferences** about the
   mental processes that lead to particular behaviours, since they can't be observed directly.

7) For example, cognitive psychologists have deduced that memory can be
   divided into short-term memory and long-term memory based on studies that
   show primacy and recency effects (see page 17). These experiments have
   lead to **theoretical models**, such as the multi-store model of memory (page 17).

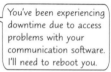

You've been experiencing
downtime due to access
problems with your
communication software.
I'll need to reboot you.

Cognitive Psychologists Use **Three** Main Research Methods

Here's a snappy little phrase to remind yourself with before you read on: '**ecological validity**' — it's the measure
of how much the result of an experiment reflects what would happen in **natural settings**. If a result has **low**
ecological validity, it might work fine in the lab. But try to use it to explain real-life behaviour, and you'll find
yourself up the creek without a paddle. And no one wants that.

1 — Laboratory Experiments

A lot of research in cognitive psychology happens in
laboratories. This is very **scientific** and reliable as it is
possible to have great control over variables in a lab.
However, often this type of research doesn't tell us much
about the real world — it has **low ecological validity**.

2 — Field Experiments

Field experiments take place in a **natural**
situation (e.g. studies of memory or
attention in a school environment), so they
have more ecological validity, but there's
less control of most of the variables.

3 — Natural Experiments

Natural experiments involve making observations of a **naturally occurring situation**.
The experimenter has little control of the variables, and participants can't be randomly
assigned to conditions. Natural experiments have **high ecological validity**, but they're
not massively reliable, as **uncontrolled** (or **confounding**) variables can affect the results.

The **Principles** of the Cognitive Approach

Cognitive psychologists have outlined several general principles:

- **Our mental systems have a limited capacity** — The amount of information that can be processed
  will be influenced by how demanding the task is and how much other information is being processed.

- **A control mechanism oversees all mental processes** — This will require more processing power for
  new tasks, leaving less available for everything else.

- **There is a two-way flow of information** — We take in information from the world, process it, and react
  to it. We also use our knowledge and experiences to understand the world.

The Cognitive Approach

Cognitive Psychology Developed as the *Computer Age Developed*

As computers developed in the 1950s and 1960s, the analogy between the human brain and a computer was formed.

1) People began to see similarities in how computers and humans make sense of information.

2) Computer terms are often used in cognitive psychology.
   Cognitive psychologists use **computer models** to represent particular features of the human mind.

- The brain is described as a **processor** (the thing that makes things happen) — it has data **input** into it, and **output** from it.
- Some parts of the brain form **networks** (interconnected parts).
- Some parts can work **sequentially** (info travels along just one path). This means one process must finish before another starts. This occurs in more demanding, or unknown tasks.
- And they can work in **parallel** too (info travels to and fro along lots of paths at the same time). This is more likely to happen for tasks which are familiar.

As well as computer models, theoretical models are used to explain and predict behaviour.

3) The computer and human systems follow the **same** route — data input, processing and data output. For example:

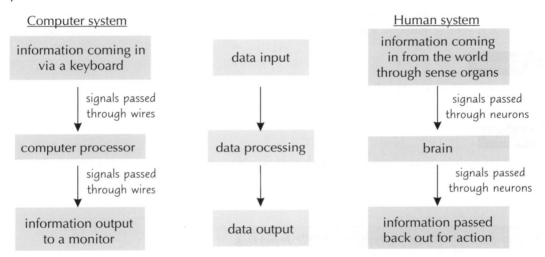

Be careful though... there are **differences** between humans and computers that make computer models less useful:

- Humans are often influenced by **emotional** and **motivational** factors — something computers aren't affected by.
- Humans have an **unlimited** but **unreliable** memory, whereas computers have a limited but reliable memory.
- Humans also have **free will** (the ability to choose between decisions) which computers don't.

Practice Questions

Q1 Outline three research methods that cognitive psychologists might use.

Q2 Outline the principles of the cognitive approach.

Exam Question

Q1 a) Describe how cognitive psychologists use computer and theoretical models to explain mental processes. [6 marks]

   b) Evaluate the use of computer and theoretical models to explain mental processes. [6 marks]

Overloaded with information? Processor running slowly? Time to reboot...

It's a big ol' technical world out there, so it kind of makes sense that cognitive psychologists compare our brains to a computer. But just be wary of ignoring all our emotional stuff. If a computer started to cry, it'd electrocute itself...

The Cognitive Approach

More on the cognitive approach? It really is your lucky day...

A **Schema** Helps You **Organise** All the Information You Know

A **schema** contains all the information you know about an object, action or concept — e.g. the schema of a human face contains the information that a face has two eyes, a mouth and a nose, and the schema of riding a bike contains all the movements you'd need to make. Schemas help you to **organise** and **interpret** information and experiences.

- When information is **consistent** with a schema, it is **assimilated** into the schema. For example, a child's schema for an apple may be an edible, green, hard sphere. Everytime the child sees a green apple, the experience is assimilated and the schema is strengthened.
- When information is **inconsistent** with a schema, **accommodation** occurs and the schema has to **change** in order to **resolve** the problem. So if a child sees a red apple, their apple schema has to **accommodate** this new information — it becomes an edible, hard sphere that is either green or red.

There are lots of different **types** of schema:

Role Schemas

These are ideas about the behaviour which is expected from someone in a certain role, setting or situation. E.g. your schema for a doctor might be someone who is intelligent, respectable, sensible, etc.

Event Schemas

These are also called **scripts**. They contain information about what happens in a situation. E.g. when you go to a restaurant you know you'll usually need to read a menu and place an order.

Self Schemas

These contain information about **ourselves** based on physical characteristics and personality, as well as beliefs and values. Self schemas can affect how you act — e.g. if your self-schema says that you are health-conscious, you are likely to eat well and exercise regularly.

There are Some **Problems** with **Schemas**

Sometimes schemas can **stop** people from **learning** new information.

For example, **prejudice** and **stereotypes** can be an **outcome** of schemas. A schema which holds expectations or beliefs about a certain subgroup of people may bias the way we process incoming information. This means we may be more likely to **pay attention** to information we can **easily assimilate**, and ignore information that would involve changing our schemas to **accommodate**.

Bartlett Investigated **Schemas**

Bartlett (1932) was one of the first psychologists to test and illustrate the idea of schemas.

	Bartlett (1932) — The War of the Ghosts
Method:	English participants were asked to read a Native American folk tale, called 'The War of the Ghosts'. It was an **unfamiliar** story, full of strange and unusual names, ideas and objects. It also had a different structure to your average English story. The participants were asked to **recall** the story after different lengths of time.
Results:	All of the participants changed the story to fit their own schemas. The details in the story became more English, the story started to contain elements of English culture, and details and emotions were added. As the length of time between hearing and recalling the story increased, the amount of information remembered became a lot less.
Conclusion:	People use their own schemas to help interpret and remember the world around them.
Evaluation:	This study was conducted in a laboratory, so it lacks **ecological validity**. But it was highly influential at the time as it paved the way for further cognitive research.

The Cognitive Approach

The Emergence of **Cognitive Neuroscience**

1) Although the cognitive approach started in the 1950s and 1960s, it wasn't until the 1970s that the influence of neuroscience really took hold. With modern brain imaging techniques and procedures, **cognitive neuroscience** started to emerge.

2) Cognitive neuroscience is an approach in psychology which **maps** human **behaviour** to **brain function**. Brain-imaging techniques allow psychologists to discover when and where things happen in the brain in relation to people's behaviour at the time.

Gerry was super excited to hear about developments in cognitive neuroscience.

Cognitive Neuroscience Uses Lots of *Different* Methods

Cognitive neuroscientists use a variety of methods to study cognition. They include:

- **lesion studies** –– looking at people with brain damage to see how behaviour is affected (see page 55).
- **electrophysiology** — using electric and magnetic fields to measure brain activity and brain waves (see page 54).
- **neuroimaging** — pinpointing areas of the brain which are active when a task is performed. For example, PET scans (p.54) have been used to show the brain areas that are most active during memory tasks.

The Cognitive Approach Has **Strengths** and **Weaknesses**

Strengths
- It considers **mental processes** which are often overlooked in the other approaches.
- It has had a big **influence** on the development of **therapies**, e.g. cognitive behaviour therapy (page 69).

Weaknesses
- Research is often carried out in **artificial situations** (laboratories, using computer models) and the role of emotion and influence from other people is often ignored. For these reasons some argue that the results aren't valid in the real world.
- Cognitive psychology fails to take **individual differences** into account by assuming that all of us process stuff in exactly the same way.

Practice Questions

Q1 What is a 'schema'?

Q2 Describe two types of schema.

Q3 Give one research method used in cognitive neuroscience.

Exam Questions

Q1 What is cognitive neuroscience? Illustrate your answer with an example. [4 marks]

Q2 Read the item and then answer the question that follows.

> Jo took her daughter to the zoo. When her daughter saw the zebras, she pointed and said "horse".

Use schemas to explain how Jo's daughter made this mistake. [2 marks]

The next thing you'll know, they'll be reading minds...

Cognitive neuroscience is making a big impact in the world of psychology. So be careful — there'll soon be an app on your phone which will know what you're thinking. But when that happens, remember one thing. You saw it here first. CGP — leading the way in cognitive neuroscience and technology. Sort of.

The Biological Approach — The Role of Genetics

The biological approach is all about looking at how genes, neurotransmitters and other squidgy bits cause behaviour. It's kind of a bit like Biology at school, except you won't have to dissect anything...

There are Three Basic **Assumptions** of the Biological Approach

1) Human behaviour can be explained by looking at biological stuff such as **hormones**, **genetics**, **evolution** and the **nervous system**.

2) In theory, if we can explain all behaviour using **biological causes**, unwanted behaviour could be **modified** or **removed** using **biological treatments** such as medication for mental illness.

3) Experimental research conducted using **animals** can inform us about human behaviour and biological influences, because we share a lot of biological similarities.

Genetics is Used to Explain Behaviour

First of all, here's a speedy recap of the basic genetic knowledge that will be handy to know:

1) At conception, the egg and sperm join up to give a total of **46 chromosomes**.

2) Each chromosome is made up of a coil of **DNA**, which in turn is made up of loads and loads of **genes**.

3) The genes contain the information that make us **unique** in appearance (e.g. hair, skin and eye colour).

4) However, genes are also relevant in psychology, as they are important in the **development** of the **brain**, and therefore have a role in our **behaviour**.

> **Darwin's theory of evolution** suggests that over time, individuals who are **better adapted** to their environment through having **better genes** are more likely to survive to reproduce and pass on their useful genes. Those who are **less well-adapted** will be less likely to survive to reproduce and pass on their genes. Eventually, their less useful genes will be eliminated from the gene pool for that species. Through this process of **natural selection**, early humans **became better adapted** to their environments. For instance, behaviours such as **phobias** and **aggression** may have evolved because of the survival advantage they gave.

5) The **genotype** of a person is the genes they have. The **phenotype** of a person is the characteristics their genes produce — for example, hair colour, eye colour, etc.

Genetics Can Explain **Psychological Traits**

Faulty genes are known to cause some diseases that have psychological effects, e.g. Huntington's disease that leads to a deterioration of mental abilities.

Biological psychologists reckon that **genetics** can explain **"psychological traits"**. These are things like gender behaviour (things that men and women do differently), intelligence, personality and sexual orientation.

Declan was not happy to learn that 'genes' and 'jeans' were very different things.

They also study genetics to see which genes make some people **more likely** to develop things like **mental illness** or **addictions**.

Twin studies and **adoption studies** are useful for investigating these areas.

The Biological Approach — The Role of Genetics

Research Has Looked at the Genetic Basis of Mental Illnesses

Schizophrenia is a mental illness which has been studied a lot in psychology.
Twin studies and **adoption studies** have highlighted the possible role of genetics.

Twin Studies

Identical twins share **100%** of their genes. So in theory, if schizophrenia has a purely **genetic basis** and if one twin suffers from schizophrenia, then the other twin will too. **Non-identical twins** share **50%** of their genes, so the risk of both suffering should be lower.

Gottesman (1991) — A meta-analysis of twin studies

Method: Gottesman carried out a meta-analysis of approximately 40 twin studies.

Results: It was found that having an **identical twin** with schizophrenia gave you a **48%** chance of developing the condition. This reduced to **17%** in **non-identical twins**.

Conclusion: Schizophrenia has a strong **genetic basis**.

Evaluation: The meta-analysis was carried out on field studies, giving the research **high ecological validity**. Because identical twins share 100% of their genes, it might be expected that both twins would always suffer from the same conditions. The fact that both twins had developed schizophrenia in only about half of the cases means that **another factor** must also be involved. Identical twins tend to be treated more similarly than non-identical twins, and so the **family environment** might play a large role.

Adoption Studies

Adoption studies have also provided evidence for a **genetic basis** of schizophrenia.

Heston (1966) — An adoption study of schizophrenia

Method: 47 adopted children whose biological mothers had schizophrenia were studied. The control group consisted of 50 adopted children whose biological mothers didn't suffer from schizophrenia. The children were followed up as adults and were interviewed and given intelligence and personality tests.

Results: Of the experimental group, 5 of the 47 became schizophrenic, compared to 0 in the control group. Another 4 of the experimental group were classified as borderline schizophrenic by the raters.

Conclusion: The study supports the view that schizophrenia has a **genetic basis**.

Evaluation: Interview data can be unreliable and affected by **social desirability bias**. However, interviews are a good way of getting data in a **naturalistic way**. The adopted children whose mothers didn't suffer from any conditions might have not shown any symptoms of schizophrenia **yet** — it can't be completely ruled out.

Practice Questions

Q1 Define 'genotype' and 'phenotype'.

Q2 Describe one study which supports the argument for the genetic basis of mental illness.

Exam Questions

Q1 Complete the following sentence:
The biological model assumes behaviour can be determined by
  A genetics   **B** role models   **C** operant conditioning   **D** classical conditioning   [1 mark]

Q2 Discuss the role of genetics within the biological approach.   [8 marks]

Flares, skinny, straight leg, boyfriend fit... it's all about the genes...

Your genes help make you who you are. And not just someone with a keen fashion sense. Don't forget that there are lots of different types of jeans, for every different shape and size. So find the ones that suit you best.

The Biological Approach — Brain Structure

Biological psychologists also reckon that behaviour can be determined by brain structure. Nowadays they use scanning techniques to look at people's brains and try to link structures and activity to various behaviours.

At First it was *Trickier* to *Investigate Brain Structure* and *Function*

Before brain-scanning techniques were developed, psychologists relied on **case studies** of people who had experienced a **brain injury** or had **brain operations**. If the person had brain damage in a **specific area** and also a **change in behaviour**, the assumption could be made that the two were related.

For example, in 1848 **Phineas Gage** had damage to part of his **frontal lobe** after an explosion at work resulted in an iron bar going straight through his head (ouch). After the accident he was **less organised**, and **more impulsive**, and experienced personality changes including **increased aggression**. This led to the belief that this area of the brain is responsible for these behaviours. However, this is a case study of only one person, and so isn't **representative** of the population, which leads to problems with **generalising** the results.

But psychologists can't just sit around waiting for people with brain injuries to turn up so they can study them. For one thing, studies like that aren't conducted in **controlled** circumstances, so they're less **scientific**. And **ethically** we can't **deliberately** inflict this type of brain injury on humans. **Non-human animals** have been used to study brain structure and behaviour, but the differences between non-human animal brains and human brains mean that the results may not be that useful when we apply them to **human behaviour** (and there are still **ethics** to be considered when animals are used in research). So ideally psychologists could do with another way of studying brain structure and behaviour — ah-ha, that leads us nicely on to **brain scans**...

Brain Scans Can Help Examine Patterns of Brain Activity and Anatomy

There are five basic techniques used:

1) **PET scans** (positron emission tomography — not what happens in the vets) show which parts of the brain are **active** during different tasks. By studying PET scans, we can link certain areas of the brain with particular **functions**. They also allow us to see where the brain is most active when we are **thinking** about certain things. They show average activity over a 60-second period, not moment by moment.
2) **CAT scans** detect **damaged** parts of the brain, tumours and blood clots. Brain **structure** is shown, not function.
3) **MRI scans** detect small tumours and provide **detailed** information about **structure**.
4) **Functional MRI scans** provide **structural** and **functional** information.
5) **SQUID magnetometry** produces accurate images of brain **activity** by measuring the magnetic fields generated when neurons are activated. However, outside sources of magnetism can affect measurements.

There's Evidence from *MRI* Scans to Show *Changes* in Brain Structure

Maguire et al (2000) — A study of taxi drivers' brains

Method:	In a **natural experiment**, MRI scans from 16 licensed male London taxi drivers were compared with a control group who had never driven taxis. All of the participants were in good general, neurological and psychiatric health, and had an average age of 44. All of the taxi drivers had been working for at least 18 months.
Results:	The average size of the right posterior hippocampus was **significantly larger** in the taxi driver group compared to the control group. Additionally, the increased size was relative to the length of time the taxi driver had been working — the **longer** they'd been working, the **larger** their right posterior hippocampus.
Conclusion:	The hippocampus is responsible for storing a spatial representation of the environment — it seems that the specific navigational demands on the taxi drivers have resulted in physical change.
Evaluation:	The findings of the study could be used to help those with brain injuries as it shows that the size of structures within the brain can be influenced through cognitive activity. This means **rehabilitation** could be tailored to the specific needs of individuals and their injuries. The study had a good level of **control** and could be **replicated**, which increases its **reliability**. The **sample size** is small though, and the results can only be **generalised** to male taxi drivers in London. Also, the results can't be generalised to **other areas** of the brain.

The Biological Approach — Brain Structure

Brain Structure Has Been Investigated in **Several Areas** of Psychology

1) **Aggression** — Bard and Mountcastle (1948) found that lesioning (i.e. damaging) areas of the brains of **cats** led to changes in levels of **aggression**. Their research suggests that the **hypothalamus** and **amygdala** are involved in aggression.

2) **Memory** — in a case study, Milner et al (1957) found that **HM** was unable to use his long-term memory effectively, suggesting that the **hippocampus** has an important role here (see page 17).

3) **Psychopathology** — Szeszko et al (1995) found differences in the **prefrontal cortex** when comparing people with and without **schizophrenia**, suggesting a relationship between them.

Neurochemistry Might Also Influence Behaviour

Neurochemistry is all about the **nervous system** and **neurotransmitters**.
The **biological approach** looks at the role they might play in explaining behaviour.

- Too much or too little of a particular **neurotransmitter** may produce psychological disorders, e.g. an increased level of **dopamine** is linked to schizophrenia. **Drugs** like cocaine, which increase dopamine levels, can lead to schizophrenia-like symptoms.
- Some biological psychologists investigate the impact **neurotransmitters** have on behaviour. You can read more about what they do on pages 56 and 59.

The Biological Approach Has **Strengths** and **Weaknesses**

Strengths:

1) The approach can provide **evidence** to support or disprove a theory — it's a very **scientific** approach.

2) If a biological cause can be found for mental health problems or for unwanted behaviour such as aggression, then **biological treatments** can be developed to help individuals.

Weaknesses:

1) The approach doesn't take into account the influence of people's **environment**, their **family**, **childhood experiences** or their **social situation**. Other approaches see these as being important factors in explaining behaviour.

2) Using a biological explanation for negative behaviour can lead to individuals or groups avoiding taking **personal** or **social responsibility** for their behaviour.

Practice Questions

Q1 What research method did Maguire et al (2000) use?
Q2 Name one area of psychology which has been investigated by looking at brain structure.
Q3 Which brain structures did Bard and Mountcastle (1948) suggest are involved in aggression?

Exam Questions

Q1 Read the item and then answer the question that follows.

> Alicia suffered a stroke last year that caused some damage to part of her brain. She has since become more careless, irritable and confused.

Discuss how a biological psychologist might explain Alicia's behaviour. [2 marks]

Q2 Describe the influence of neurochemistry on behaviour. [4 marks]

Imagine what your brain will look like when it's full of all this goodness...

That's it for the approaches. Done. Finis. Over. But, before you go out and celebrate, make sure you know it all inside out. It's an important section as it makes all the other bits of Psychology make much more sense.

The Nervous System

*Biopsychology is really quite exciting. Biology **and** psychology. I know, right — what more could you want...*

Biopsychology Uses Biology to Explain Behaviour

Biopsychology is all about how **biology** influences **behaviour**. Biopsychologists study things like the **nervous system**, **neurotransmitters** and **hormones** — and that means you should too. Sorry about that. First up, the **nervous system**...

The **Nervous System** Has **Two** Key Parts

1) Your nervous system is what allows you to **respond** to changes in your **environment** (stimuli).
   It also allows you to **coordinate** your actions.

2) **Receptors** detect stimuli and **effectors** bring about a response to a stimulus.
   Effectors include **muscle cells** and cells found in **glands**, e.g. the pancreas.

3) Receptors **communicate** with effectors via the **nervous** or **endocrine systems** (see p.60-61), or sometimes both.

4) The nervous and endocrine systems **coordinate** the response.

5) The nervous system has two parts, the **central nervous system (CNS)** and the **peripheral nervous system (PNS)**:

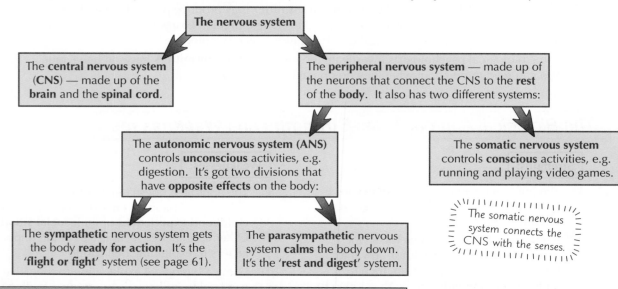

The nervous system

The **central nervous system** (**CNS**) — made up of the **brain** and the **spinal cord**.

The **peripheral nervous system** — made up of the neurons that connect the CNS to the **rest** of the **body**. It also has two different systems:

The **autonomic nervous system (ANS)** controls **unconscious** activities, e.g. digestion. It's got two divisions that have **opposite effects** on the body:

The **somatic nervous system** controls **conscious** activities, e.g. running and playing video games.

The **sympathetic** nervous system gets the body **ready for action**. It's the '**flight or fight**' system (see page 61).

The **parasympathetic** nervous system **calms** the body down. It's the '**rest and digest**' system.

The somatic nervous system connects the CNS with the senses.

The **Cells** of the Nervous System are Called **Neurons**

1) Neurons transmit information as **electrical impulses** around the body.

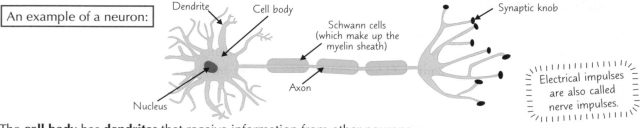

An example of a neuron:

Dendrite   Cell body   Schwann cells (which make up the myelin sheath)   Synaptic knob

Nucleus   Axon

Electrical impulses are also called nerve impulses.

2) The **cell body** has **dendrites** that receive information from other neurons.

3) This info passes along the **axon** in the form of an **electrical impulse** that ends up at a **synaptic knob**.
   The **myelin sheath** insulates the axon to speed up nervous transmission.

4) There's a small gap before the next neuron called a **synapse**.

5) **Neurotransmitters** are chemicals that are released from the synaptic knob. They pass across the synapse, to pass on the signal to the dendrites of the next neuron. (See page 58 for more on synapses.)

> Biopsychologists spend loads of time working out what different neurotransmitters do and how they can be influenced by things like **diet**, **exercise** and **drugs**. They also work out how to manipulate neurotransmitters with **medications**, to control different behaviours.
>
> For example, if a medication or diet was developed to reduce the neurotransmitters that signal stress, this could help people who get stressed out too easily.

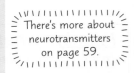

There's more about neurotransmitters on page 59.

The Nervous System

Different **Types** of **Neurons** Have Different **Roles**

Different types of neuron are involved in the transfer of information **to** and **from** the CNS.
The **structure** of these neurons differs:

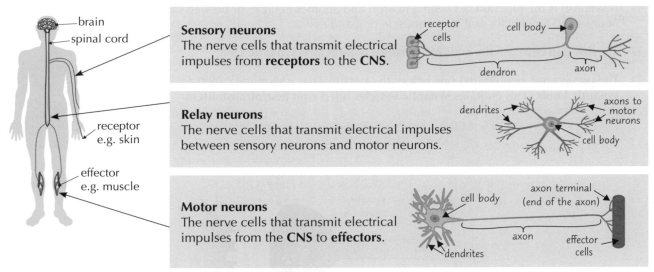

Sensory neurons
The nerve cells that transmit electrical impulses from **receptors** to the **CNS**.

Relay neurons
The nerve cells that transmit electrical impulses between sensory neurons and motor neurons.

Motor neurons
The nerve cells that transmit electrical impulses from the **CNS** to **effectors**.

The **transmission** of information to and from the CNS is shown below:

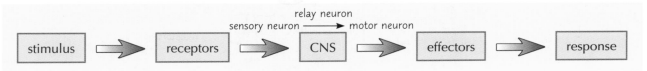

Reflexes Help Prevent **Injury**

Reflexes are fast, automatic responses to certain stimuli. They **bypass** your **conscious** brain completely — instead they go through the **spinal cord** or through an **unconscious** part of the brain. These **rapid responses** help us to **avoid damage**.

Practice Questions

Q1 What does the central nervous system (CNS) consist of?

Q2 Which branch of the autonomic nervous system (ANS) is known as the 'rest and digest' system?

Q3 Outline how information is transmitted to and from the central nervous system (CNS).

Exam Questions

Q1 Label the neuron below by putting the correct letter in each box.

A synaptic knob
B nucleus
C dendrite
D cell body
E axon

[3 marks]

Q2 Which of the following are controlled by the somatic nervous system?
A digestion   **B** breathing   **C** conscious activities   **D** unconscious activities   [1 mark]

Q3 Outline the function of sensory, relay and motor neurons.   [3 marks]

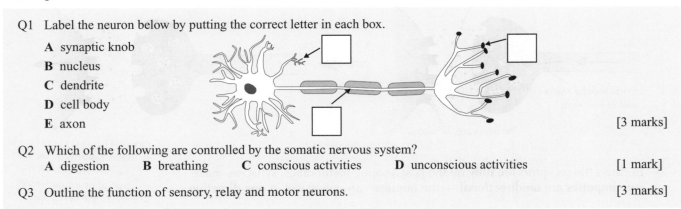

Take a deep breath and let your parasympathetic nervous system kick in...

There's a lot of biology stuff on these pages, but... DON'T PANIC. THERE IS NOTHING TO WORRY ABOUT. (Sorry — my sympathetic nervous system took over there.) Must remember... parasympathetic means calm. Ahhhh...

The Nervous System

You met neurotransmitters and synapses on page 56. Well, here's a bit more about them. It's your lucky day...

A **Synapse** is a **Junction** Between a Neuron and the Next Cell

1) A synapse is the **junction** between a neuron and another neuron, or between a neuron and an effector cell, e.g. a muscle or gland cell.

2) The tiny **gap** between the cells at a synapse is called the **synaptic cleft**.

3) The presynaptic neuron (the one before the synapse) has a swelling called a **synaptic knob**. This contains **synaptic vesicles** filled with **neurotransmitters**.

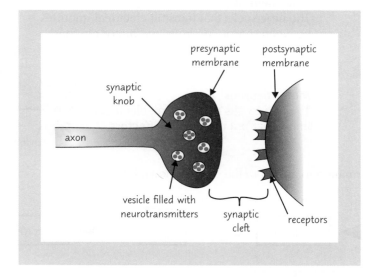

4) When an **electrical impulse** reaches the end of a neuron it causes **neurotransmitters** to be **released** into the synaptic cleft. They **diffuse across** to the **postsynaptic membrane** (the one after the synapse) and **bind** to **specific receptors**.

5) When neurotransmitters bind to receptors they might **trigger** an **electrical impulse** (in a neuron), cause **muscle contraction** (in a muscle cell), or cause a **hormone** to be **secreted** (from a gland cell).

6) Here's what happens when an electrical impulse **arrives** at a **synapse** between **two neurons**:

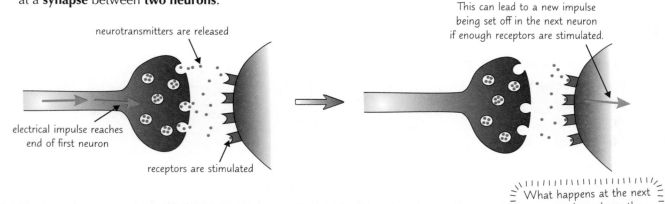

7) Because the receptors are **only** on the postsynaptic membranes, synapses make sure **impulses** are **unidirectional** — the impulse can only travel in **one direction**.

What happens at the next neuron depends on the type of neurotransmitter (see the next page).

8) Neurotransmitters are **removed** from the **cleft** so the **response** doesn't keep happening, e.g. they're taken back into the **presynaptic neuron** or they're **broken down** by **enzymes** (and the products are taken into the neuron).

The Nervous System

Neurotransmitters are **Excitatory** or **Inhibitory**

- Excitatory neurotransmitters **increase** the likelihood that an electrical impulse will be triggered in the postsynaptic neuron.

- Inhibitory neurotransmitters **decrease** the likelihood that an electrical impulse will be triggered in the postsynaptic neuron.

Mum couldn't help wishing Harry had a few more inhibitory neurotransmitters.

Some **Neurotransmitters** Come Up a Lot in **Psychology**

There are lots of different neurotransmitters, but some play a larger role than others in **human behaviour**:

Acetylcholine

This **excitatory** neurotransmitter is involved in voluntary **movement**, **memory**, **learning** and **sleep**. Too much is linked to **depression** and too little may result in **dementia**.

Dopamine

Dopamine is a neurotransmitter that helps with **movement**, **attention** and **learning**. Too much is linked to **schizophrenia**, and too little could result in **depression** and **Parkinson's disease**.

Noradrenaline

Noradrenaline is closely related to **adrenaline**. It is often associated with the 'fight or flight' response (see page 61). Too much is linked to **schizophrenia** and too little may result in **depression**.

Serotonin

Serotonin is involved in emotion, mood, sleeping and eating. Too little is linked to **depression**.

GABA

GABA is an **inhibitory** neurotransmitter. Too little GABA is linked to **anxiety disorders**.

Practice Questions

Q1 What is a synapse?

Q2 How do synapses ensure that nerve impulses are unidirectional?

Q3 Give one way that neurotransmitters are removed from the synaptic cleft.

Q4 Explain the difference between an excitatory and inhibitory neurotransmitter.

Q5 Name four different neurotransmitters.

Exam Questions

Q1 Outline how information is transmitted between two neurons. [6 marks]

Q2 Look at the synapse to the right and answer the following questions.

a) What is the name of Structure X?

    A synaptic knob
    B synaptic cleft
    C receptor
    D vesicle
    E postsynaptic membrane [1 mark]

b) What is released from Structure X? [1 mark]

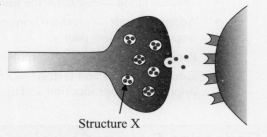

Structure X

Talk about being a bit of a noradrenaline junkie...

Yep, that's me. Someone who truly loves rollercoasters, extreme ironing Synd Psychology revision. Give me a dose of noradrenaline any day. In fact, some days, my heart gets racing just at the thought of those joyful exams which'll be here before you know it. Hmmm... maybe you should start to learn some of this stuff now. Go on — it won't bite...

The Endocrine System

Some days you might wake up and not want to do any Psychology revision. Don't blame it on Psychology. Blame it on your hormones — they can account for a lot you know...

The **Endocrine System** Sends Information as **Chemical Signals**

1) The **endocrine system** (also known as the hormonal system) involves **glands** and **hormones**:

> A **gland** is a group of cells that are specialised to **secrete** a useful substance, such as a **hormone**. E.g. the **pancreas** secretes **insulin**.
>
> Hormones are '**chemical messengers**'. Many hormones are **proteins** or **peptides**, e.g. **insulin**. Some hormones are **steroids**, e.g. **progesterone**.

2) **Hormones** are **secreted** when a **gland** is **stimulated**:

> Glands can be **stimulated** by a **change** in **concentration** of a specific **substance** (sometimes **another hormone**).
> They can also be **stimulated** by **electrical impulses**.

3) Hormones **diffuse directly into** the **blood**, then they're **taken** around the body by the **circulatory system**.

4) They **diffuse out** of the blood **all over** the **body**, but each hormone will only **bind** to **specific receptors** for that hormone, found on the membranes of some cells (called **target cells**).

An organ that contains target cells is called a target organ.

5) The hormones trigger a **response** in the **target cells** (the **effectors**).

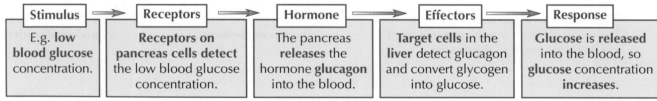

Stimulus	Receptors	Hormone	Effectors	Response
E.g. **low blood glucose** concentration.	**Receptors on pancreas cells detect** the low blood glucose concentration.	The pancreas **releases** the hormone **glucagon** into the blood.	**Target cells** in the **liver** detect glucagon and convert glycogen into glucose.	**Glucose is released** into the blood, so **glucose** concentration **increases**.

6) The **endocrine system** is responsible for regulating a large number of **bodily functions**, such as **growth**, **metabolism**, **sleep**, **reproduction**, etc. There are several major glands:

- **Hypothalamus** — it produces hormones that control the **pituitary gland**.
- **Pituitary gland** — known as the '**master gland**' because it releases hormones to control other glands in the endocrine system.
- **Pineal gland** — responsible for the production of **melatonin**, which plays a role in the control of **sleep patterns**.
- **Thyroid gland** — produces hormones such as **thyroxine**. The thyroid is responsible for controlling the body's **metabolic rate**, as well as regulating **growth** and **maturation**.
- **Parathyroid glands** — produce a hormone called the **parathyroid hormone**. This helps control the levels of minerals such as **calcium** within the body.
- **Thymus gland** — regulates the **immune system**.
- **Adrenal glands** — produce hormones such as **adrenaline**. Responsible for the '**fight or flight**' response (see next page).
- **Pancreas** — releases the hormones **insulin** and **glucagon**, which regulate **blood sugar** level.
- **Gonads (ovaries and testes)** — produce sex hormones, e.g. **testosterone** and **oestrogen**. These are important in **reproduction** and the **development of sex organs** and **secondary sexual characteristics**.

Endocrine System Communication is Slower, Long-lasting and Widespread

- Hormones **aren't** released directly onto their target cells — they must **travel** in the **blood** to get there. This means that chemical communication (by hormones) is **slower** than electrical communication (by nerves).
- They **aren't broken down as quickly** as neurotransmitters, so the **effects** of hormones can **last** for much **longer**.
- Hormones are transported **all over** the **body**, so the response may be **widespread** if the target cells are widespread.

The Endocrine System

The **Hypothalamus** Prepares You for '**Fight** or **Flight**'

When the body is **threatened** (e.g. by a danger such as a giant face-licking millipede) it responds by **preparing for action** (e.g. for fighting or running away). This response is called the '**fight** or **flight**' response. The **hypothalamus** helps coordinate this response. Here's how...

The activation of the '**fight** or **flight**' response

1) In the **initial shock response**, the **hypothalamus** triggers activity in the **sympathetic branch** of the **autonomic nervous system** (**ANS**).

2) This stimulates the **adrenal medulla** within the **adrenal glands**, which releases **adrenaline** and **noradrenaline** into the bloodstream.

3) These hormones affect the body in several ways, including:

   - **Blood pressure** and **heart rate** increase to get blood quickly to areas of the body where it's needed for activity.
   - **Digestion decreases** so that blood can be directed to the brain and muscles.
   - **Muscles** become more **tense** so that the body is physically responsive.
   - **Perspiration increases** so that the body can cool down.
   - **Breathing rate increases** so that more oxygen can be sent to the muscles.
   - **Pupil size increases** so more light can enter the eye to allow for clearer vision.
   - **Salivation decreases** as the digestive system isn't needed.

   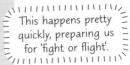
   This happens pretty quickly, preparing us for 'fight or flight'.

4) The result of these changes is that the body is **ready to use energy** to deal with the stressful situation, e.g. running away from the rhino that's escaped from the zoo.

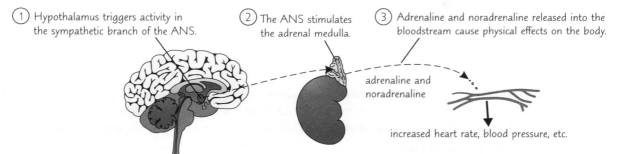

① Hypothalamus triggers activity in the sympathetic branch of the ANS.

② The ANS stimulates the adrenal medulla.

③ Adrenaline and noradrenaline released into the bloodstream cause physical effects on the body.

adrenaline and noradrenaline

increased heart rate, blood pressure, etc.

Practice Questions

Q1 What is the endocrine system also known as?

Q2 Describe the role of the pituitary gland.

Q3 Which endocrine gland is responsible for regulating blood sugar level?

Exam Questions

Q1 Outline how hormones allow communication within the body. [6 marks]

Q2 Read the item below, then answer the question that follows.

> When Anita saw a spider, her heart rate increased, she started to sweat and she began breathing rapidly.

Discuss how adrenaline can explain Anita's reaction. [6 marks]

Let's get ready to rumble...

If you've ever had that panicky feeling just before going into an exam, or whilst paragliding over a bubbling volcano (you never know), that'll be your hypothalamus kicking into action. It's kind of nice that it gets you ready for these sorts of things. Isn't your body a marvellous thing? It's always good to be prepared, as the Scouts might say...

Defining Abnormality

Defining what's abnormal is easy — it's just what's not normal. But what's normal...?

Abnormality Can be Described as **Deviation from Social Norms**

1) All societies have their **standards** of behaviour and attitudes. Deviating from these can be seen as abnormal.

2) But **cultures vary**, so there isn't one universal set of social 'rules'.

3) One problem with defining abnormality as deviation from social norms is that it can be used to **justify** the removal of 'unwanted' people from a society. For example, people opposing a particular political regime could be said to be abnormal.

4) Another limitation of defining abnormality as deviation from social norms is that what is considered acceptable or abnormal can **change over time**. For example, as recently as 1974, homosexuality was classified in the **Diagnostic and Statistical Manual of Mental Disorders (DSM)** (see page 64) as a **disorder**. However, the diagnosis was dropped because it was found that homosexuality **wasn't as infrequent** as previously thought, and that homosexuals don't differ from heterosexuals in terms of **psychological well-being**.

Abnormality Can also be Described as **Deviation from Statistical Norms**

Abnormality can also be seen as statistically rare behaviour — this can be expressed in terms of the **normal distribution**:

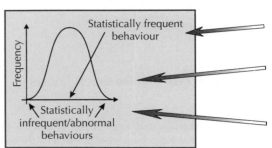

People who behave in the average way make up the middle of the bell-shaped curve.

Those people who behave 'abnormally' make up the tail ends of the bell curve — this behaviour is rare (statistically infrequent).

This axis shows a numerical measure of the behaviour, e.g. the number of hand washes per week.

Not all traits show a normal distribution.

However, there are **problems** with defining abnormality simply in terms of statistical infrequency:

1) It doesn't take account of the **desirability of behaviour**, just its frequency. For example, a very high IQ is abnormal, as is a very low one, but having a high IQ is desirable whereas having a low IQ is undesirable.

2) There's **no distinction** between **rare**, **slightly odd** behaviour and **rare**, **psychologically abnormal** behaviour.

3) There's **no definite cut-off point** where normal behaviour becomes abnormal behaviour.

4) Some behaviours that are considered psychologically abnormal are quite common, e.g. mild depression. **Hassett and White (1989)** argue that you cannot use statistical infrequency to define abnormality because of this. Using the statistical infrequency idea, some disorders would not be classed as anything unusual.

Failure to Function Adequately is Another Definition of **Abnormality**

You can't function adequately if you can't cope with the demands of day-to-day life.
Various **criteria** are used for diagnosis, including:

1) **Dysfunctional behaviour** — behaviour which goes against the accepted standards of behaviour.

2) **Observer discomfort** — behaviour that causes other individuals to become uncomfortable.

3) **Unpredictable behaviour** — impulsive behaviour that seems to be uncontrollable.

4) **Irrational behaviour** — behaviour that's unreasonable and illogical.

5) **Personal distress** — being affected by emotion to an excessive degree.

If you can tick the box for **more than one** of the criteria above, the person's behaviour is considered to be **abnormal**. It does seem a bit unfair though — we've probably all done stuff that could fit under these categories at some point. People are always uncomfortable around me, but that could be because I've got fleas.

Defining Abnormality

Jahoda (1958) Identified Six Conditions Associated with Ideal Mental Health

Jahoda's six conditions were:

1) **Positive self-attitude**
2) **Self-actualisation** (realising your potential, being fulfilled)
3) **Resistance to stress**
4) **Personal autonomy** (making your own decisions, being in control)
5) **Accurate perception of reality**
6) **Adaptation to the environment**

As far as Doug was concerned, he was in control of everything he needed in life.

However, it can be **hard to meet** all the standards set in this list, and they're **subjective** (ideas of what is required for each will differ from person to person).

Also, a violent offender, for example, may have a positive self-attitude and be resistant to stress, etc. — yet society wouldn't consider them to be in good mental health.

The Idea of Ideal Mental Health Varies Across Time and Between Cultures

What's considered mentally 'healthy' at one time, wouldn't necessarily be at another.
For example, in some cultures today, it's considered **abnormal** for women to **enjoy sex** — they may be forced to have their clitoris surgically removed to prevent their enjoyment. In Victorian times here, women who enjoyed sex were deemed abnormal and hence Freud coined the term '**nymphomania**'. There's still influence from this today — there are still **double standards** about male and female sexual activity.

But the idea of 'ideal' mental health can be a useful one because it moves away from focusing on mental 'illness'.

Some Symptoms are Associated with Mental Illness

The Department of Health provides a guide to assess symptoms associated with mental illness.
To be classified as a mental illness, there should be **one or more** of the following (**not temporary**) symptoms:

1) Impairment of **intellectual functions**, such as memory and comprehension.
2) Alterations to **mood** that lead to **delusional appraisals** of the past or future, or lack of any appraisal.
3) Delusional **beliefs**, such as of persecution or jealousy.
4) Disordered **thinking** — the person may be unable to appraise their situation or communicate with others.

Practice Questions

Q1 Define abnormality using the deviation from social norms explanation.
Q2 What does Jahoda (1958) say are the six conditions associated with mental health?
Q3 Give three of the symptoms that the Department of Health uses to classify mental illness.
Q4 If someone's forgotten their trousers, should they be allowed on the bus?

Exam Questions

Q1 Outline the problems with defining abnormality in terms of deviation from social norms. [3 marks]

Q2 Outline the key features of the idea of abnormality as the failure to function adequately. [6 marks]

Q3 Discuss definitions of abnormality. [12 marks]

I'm not abnormal — I'm just a little socially deviant...

Ah, wouldn't it be easier to just be a fish... Nobody minds if you're abnormal when you're under the sea — you can swim around any way you like. You could befriend a manatee and have an adventure. The kindly sea cow — he'd never judge you for your dysfunctional and unpredictable behaviour. Yes, life is much better down where it's wetter, take it from me...

Depression, Phobias and OCD

Depression, phobias and OCD are all examples of mental health disorders. The defining characteristics of mental health disorders such as these can be found in the DSM...

Psychologists Try to **Classify** Mental Disorders

The **DSM** is the American Psychiatric Association's Diagnostic and Statistical Manual of Mental Disorders. It contains mental health disorders, and is systematically reviewed and modified in line with new research.

1) The DSM is used to classify disorders using defined **diagnostic criteria**. This includes a list of symptoms which can be used as a **tool** for diagnosis.
2) The DSM makes diagnosis **concrete and descriptive**.
3) Classifications allow data to be collected about a disorder. This can help in the development of new **treatments** and medication.
4) This type of classification has been criticised for **stigmatising** people and ignoring their 'uniqueness' by putting them in **artificial groups**.

Both Dr. Jim and Dr. Bob would defend their diagnoses to the death.

Depression is a **Mood Disorder**

Mood disorders are characterised by **strong emotions**, which can influence a person's ability to **function normally**. A mood disorder can affect a person's **perceptions**, **thinking** and **behaviour**.

Depression is one of the most **common** mood disorders. There are many types, including:

1) **Major depression (unipolar disorder)** — an **episode** of depression that can occur **suddenly**.
   - Major depression can be **reactive** — caused by **external factors**, e.g. the death of a loved one.
   - Or, it can be **endogenous** — caused by **internal factors**, e.g. neurological factors.

2) **Manic depression (bipolar disorder)** — **alternation** between two **mood extremes** (**mania** and **depression**).
   - The change in mood often occurs in regular **cycles** of days or weeks.
   - Episodes of **mania** involve **overactivity**, **rapid speech** and feeling extremely **happy** or **agitated**.
   - Episodes of **depression** involve the symptoms covered below.

Depression has Lots of **Clinical Characteristics**

People with depression can experience a **range** of possible **symptoms**:

Physical / behavioural symptoms

- **Sleep disturbances** — **insomnia** (being unable to sleep) or **hypersomnia** (sleeping a lot more than usual).
- Change in **appetite** — people may eat **more** or **less** than **usual**, and gain or lose **weight**.
- **Pain** — especially **headaches**, **joint ache** and **muscle ache**.
- Lack of **activity** — **social withdrawal** and loss of **sex drive**.

Cognitive symptoms

- Experiencing persistent **negative beliefs** about **themselves** and their **abilities**.
- **Suicidal** thoughts.
- **Slower** thought processes — **difficulty concentrating** and **making decisions**.

Affective / emotional symptoms

- Extreme feelings of **sadness**, **hopelessness** and **despair**.
- **Diurnal mood variation** — changes in mood throughout the day, e.g. feeling worse in the morning.
- **Anhedonia** — no longer **enjoying** activities or hobbies that **used** to be **pleasurable**.

For a person to be diagnosed with **major depression**, the DSM (see above) states that at least **five symptoms** must have been present nearly every day for at least **two weeks**.

Depression, Phobias and OCD

A *Phobia* is an *Irrational Fear*

A phobia is an example of an **anxiety disorder** — it's an **extreme**, **irrational fear** of a particular **object** or **situation**. The **DSM** classifies several types of phobia:

1) Specific phobias

This is a fear of specific **objects** or **situations**. There are **five** subtypes:

1) **Animal** type (also called **zoophobia**, e.g. fear of spiders)
2) **Environmental dangers** type (e.g. fear of water)
3) **Blood-injection-injury** type (e.g. fear of needles)
4) **Situational** type (e.g. fear of enclosed spaces or heights)
5) **'Other'** (any phobia that isn't covered in the categories above)

2) Agoraphobia

1) This is a fear of **open spaces**, **using public transport**, being in an **enclosed space**, **waiting in line** or **being in a crowd**, or **not being at home**.
2) It's specifically linked to the **fear** of not being able to escape or find help if an embarrassing situation arises.
3) It often involves the sufferer **avoiding the situation** in order to avoid distress.
4) It may develop as a **result** of **other phobias**, because the sufferer's afraid that they'll come across the **source** of their **fear** if they leave the house.

See page 70 for a behavioural explanation of this.

3) Social anxiety disorder (social phobia)

This is the fear of **being** in **social situations** (e.g. eating in public or talking in front of a group of people). It's usually down to the possibility of being **judged** or being **embarrassed**.

Phobias have Several *Clinical Characteristics*

The different types of phobia all have very **similar** clinical characteristics.

Cognitive symptoms	**Irrational beliefs** about the **stimulus** that causes fear. People often find it **hard** to **concentrate** because they're **preoccupied** by **anxious thoughts**.
Behavioural symptoms	**Avoiding** social situations because they cause **anxiety**. This happens especially if someone has **social anxiety disorder (social phobia)** or **agoraphobia**.
	Altering behaviour to **avoid** the feared object or situation, and trying to **escape** if it's encountered. People are often generally **restless** and **easily startled**.
Physical symptoms	Activation of the **fight or flight** response when the feared object or situation is encountered or thought about. This involves release of **adrenaline, increased heart rate** and **breathing**, and **muscle tension** (see page 61).
Emotional symptoms	**Anxiety** and a feeling of **dread**.

There are Various *Diagnostic Criteria* for *Phobias*

The **DSM** classifies a fear as a phobia if you can put a tick next to these criteria:

1) There's **significant prolonged fear** of an object or situation which lasts **more than 6 months**.
2) People experience an **anxiety response** (e.g. increased heart rate) if they're exposed to the phobic stimulus.
3) Phobias are **out of proportion** to any actual danger.
4) Sufferers go out of their way to **avoid** the phobic stimulus.
5) The phobia **disrupts** their **lives**, e.g. they avoid social situations.

Sophie did everything she could to hide her parrotophobia.

Depression, Phobias and OCD

Not quite done yet... Obsessive-compulsive disorder (OCD) is up next. Most of us have the odd obsessive thought (like checking your phone's off ten times before the exam starts) — but in OCD it's taken to extremes and affects daily life.

OCD has Two Parts

1) Obsessive-compulsive disorder has two parts — **obsessions** and **compulsions**. Most people with OCD experience obsessions and compulsions that are **linked** to each other. For example, excessive worrying about catching germs (an obsession) may lead to excessive hand-washing (a compulsion).

2) Obsessions are the **cognitive** aspect of OCD, and compulsions are the **behavioural** aspect. OCD also has an **emotional** aspect — the obsessions tend to cause people **anxiety**, and their compulsions are an attempt to relieve this.

3) Obsessive-compulsive disorder affects about **2%** of the world's population. Sufferers usually develop the disorder in their **late teens** or **early 20s**. The disorder occurs **equally in men and women** and in all **ethnic groups**.

Obsessions are the Cognitive Part of the Disorder

Obsessions are **intrusive** and **persistent thoughts**, **images** and **impulses**. They are the **internal** aspect of OCD. They can range from worrying that you left the oven on to worrying that you might kill your parents. For thoughts like these to be **classified** as obsessions, the **DSM** (see page 64) outlines the following criteria:

- **Persistent** and **reoccurring** thoughts, images or impulses that are **unwanted** and cause **distress** to the person experiencing them. For example, imagining that you've left the door unlocked and burglars are rampaging through your house.

  In most people, these thoughts cause anxiety and distress.

- The person actively tries to **ignore** the thoughts, images or impulses but is **unable to**.

- The obsessions have not been caused by **other physiological substances**, such as drugs.

Compulsions are Repetitive Actions

- Compulsions are **physical** or **mental repetitive actions**. They are the **external** aspect of OCD.

- For example, **checking** the door is locked nine times or repeating a certain **phrase** or **prayer** to **neutralise** an unwanted thought.

- The problem is that the action only reduces the anxiety caused by an obsession for a **short time**, which means that the obsession starts up again.

- The **DSM** uses the following diagnostic criteria:

  1) The person **repeats physical behaviours** or **mental acts** that relate to an obsession. Sometimes the person has rules that they must follow strictly. For example, a rule that you must check the door is locked ten times before you can leave home.

  2) The compulsions are meant to **reduce anxiety** or **prevent** a feared situation — in reality they're **excessive** or **wouldn't actually stop** a dreaded situation.

  3) The compulsions have not been caused by **other physiological substances**, such as drugs.

No matter how many times he checked, the doctor still couldn't prove who'd eaten his stash of lollipops.

The DSM states that if the obsessions or compulsions last **at least one hour each day** this is an indication of a **clinical case** of OCD. Another indication of OCD is if the obsessions and compulsions **interfere** with a person's ability to maintain a relationship, hold down a job or take part in social activities.

Depression, Phobias and OCD

There are Several Types of OCD Behaviours

There are several common types of OCD behaviours. Here are four:

1) **Checking** — includes checking that the lights are off or that you have your purse or wallet.

2) **Contamination** — this involves a fear of catching germs by, say, going to a restaurant, touching door handles, shaking hands or using public toilets.

3) **Hoarding** — keeping useless or worn-out objects, such as old newspapers or junk mail.

4) **Symmetry and orderliness** — getting objects lined up 'just right', such as having all the tins in your food cupboard facing exactly the same way, or everything on your desk arranged in a neat order in the right places.

Practice Questions

Q1 What's the difference between major depression and manic depression?

Q2 What is anhedonia?

Q3 What are the five subtypes of specific phobias?

Q4 Outline the diagnostic criteria for phobias.

Q5 Give an example of an obsession.

Q6 Give an example of a compulsion.

Exam Questions

Q1 Read the item below and answer the questions that follow.

> Since Jonathan lost his job six months ago he has had low moods and has been having difficulty sleeping. He describes how he is feeling:
>
> > 'I don't get any pleasure from things any more. I used to go to the cinema or meet up with friends at the weekend, but now I don't want to go out because I know I won't enjoy it and I'll just drag other people down. I'm looking for a new job but I don't have the right skills for the jobs that are advertised. I don't think I'll ever find anything.'

    a) Outline **two** emotional characteristics of depression that you can identify in Jonathan's description.   [2 marks]

    b) Outline one cognitive characteristic of depression that is **not** mentioned in Jonathan's account.   [1 mark]

Q2 Outline one cognitive characteristic and one emotional characteristic of phobias.   [2 marks]

Q3 Read the item below, then answer the questions that follow.

> Peter suffers from intrusive thoughts that he will cause an accident while driving his car. Before driving he repeatedly checks that his seat belt is correctly fastened. Peter feels he must begin his drive to work at a precise time, and he is unable to leave the house if he misses this departure time.

    a) Outline a cognitive characteristic of OCD that you can identify from the description of Peter's experience.   [1 mark]

    b) With reference to the item above, discuss the interaction between the behavioural, emotional and cognitive characteristics of OCD.   [6 marks]

Doctor, Doctor, I'm having unwanted thoughts about revision...

OCD isn't all about checking and straightening — intrusive thoughts can be violent and upsetting, and they often cause anxiety. This anxiety is the emotional aspect of OCD, along with obsessions (cognitive) and compulsions (behavioural). On top of that, you also need to know the emotional, cognitive and behavioural aspects of depression and of phobias. Chin up...

The Cognitive Approach to Depression

The cognitive explanation of depression basically rests on the idea that disorders happen because of faulty thinking. There are other explanations for depression, and other treatments, but you just need to know the cognitive stuff. Phew.

The **Cognitive** Model of Abnormality Concentrates on **Thoughts** and **Beliefs**

The **cognitive approach** assumes that behaviours are controlled by **thoughts** and **beliefs**. So, irrational thoughts and beliefs cause abnormal behaviours.

There are several models that explain how **faulty cognitions** can lead to depression. For example:

The cognitive approach is covered in detail in Section Four.

Ellis's ABC model

1) **Ellis (1962)** proposed the '**ABC model**'.

2) The model claims that disorders begin with an **activating event (A)** (e.g. a failed exam), leading to a **belief (B)** about why this happened.

3) This may be rational (e.g. 'I didn't prepare well enough'), or irrational (e.g. 'I'm too stupid to pass exams').

4) The belief leads to a **consequence (C)**. Rational beliefs produce adaptive (appropriate) consequences (e.g. more revision). Irrational beliefs produce maladaptive (bad and inappropriate) consequences (e.g. getting depressed).

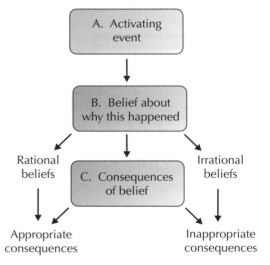

A. Activating event
→
B. Belief about why this happened
Rational beliefs — C. Consequences of belief — Irrational beliefs
Appropriate consequences / Inappropriate consequences

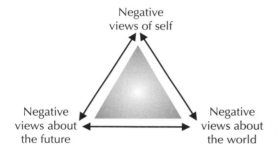

Negative views of self
Negative views about the future
Negative views about the world

Beck's negative triad

Beck (1963) identified a '**negative triad**' of automatic thoughts linked to **depression** — negative views about:

1) **themselves** (e.g. that they can't succeed at anything),

2) the **world** (e.g. that they must be successful to be a good person),

3) the **future** (e.g. that nothing will change).

The **Cognitive** Explanation of **Depression** Has **Strengths** and **Weaknesses**

Strengths:

1) The cognitive model offers a **useful** approach to depression because it considers the role of **thoughts** and **beliefs**, which are greatly involved in problems like depression.

2) Hollon and Kendall (1980) developed the **Automatic Thoughts Questionnaire (ATQ)** to measure the **negative thinking** associated with depression. **Harrell and Ryon (1983)** used the ATQ to compare negative thinking in 114 depressed and non-depressed participants. The **depressed** participants scored **significantly higher** (more negative thinking) than the other groups, supporting a **correlation** between negative thinking and depression.

3) Cognitive therapies have often **successfully treated** depression (see next page).

Strengths: Looks good in pink.

Weaknesses: Only has half a pair of trousers.

Weaknesses:

1) Faulty cognitions may simply be the **consequence** of depression rather than its cause. For example, depression may be caused by a chemical imbalance in the brain, which causes people to think very negatively.

2) The person could begin to feel like he or she is to **blame** for their problems.

The Cognitive Approach to Depression

CBT Tries to Change Faulty Cognitions

Cognitive therapies are used to treat a range of conditions, but they're particularly helpful for things like depression.

Cognitive behaviour therapy (CBT) aims to **identify** and **change** the patient's **faulty cognitions**.
The idea is that patients learn how to **notice** negative thoughts when they have them, and **test** how accurate they are.
This is generally what happens during CBT:

1) The therapist and client **identify** the client's faulty **cognitions** (thoughts and beliefs).

2) The therapist then tries to **help** the client see that these cognitions aren't true, e.g. that the client doesn't always fail at what they do.

3) Together, they then set **goals** to think in more positive or adaptive ways, e.g. focusing on things the client has succeeded at and trying to build on them.

4) Although the client may occasionally need to look back to past experiences, the treatment mainly focuses on the **present situation**.

5) Therapists sometimes encourage their clients to keep a **diary** — they can record their thought patterns, feelings and actions.

Stuart's faulty cognition had led to a disastrous footwear decision.

Advantages of CBT

- CBT **empowers** patients — it puts them in charge of their own treatment by teaching them **self-help strategies**. This means there are **fewer ethical issues** than with other therapies like drug therapy.

- **DeRubeis et al (2005)** compared **CBT** and **drug therapy** as depression treatments in a placebo-controlled trial. Both treatments were **more effective than the placebo** after 8 weeks. Generally the two therapies were similarly effective, but CBT may have been **less effective than drug therapy** in cases where therapists **lacked experience**.

- **Hollon et al (2005)** compared participants from DeRubeis et al's (2005) study after they were **withdrawn** from treatment (CBT and drug treatment), with participants who **continued** drug treatment. Participants **withdrawn from CBT** were **significantly less likely** than patients **withdrawn from drug treatment** to have **relapsed** after one year, and **no more likely** to have relapsed than patients who **continued** drug treatment.

- **Brandsma et al (1978)** found that **CBT** is particularly effective for people who put a lot of **pressure** on themselves and feel **guilty** about being **inadequate**.

CBT might be expensive initially, but if it reduces relapse then it may cost less overall. Also, if people need less time off work and are able to contribute more to society, it's better for the economy in the long run (see page 95).

Disadvantages of CBT

- Cognitive therapies may take a long **time** and be **costly**. They may be more effective when **combined** with other approaches, e.g. drug therapy.

- As **DeRubeis et al (2005)** found, CBT may only be effective if the therapist is **experienced**. Patients whose therapists are still gaining this experience may be better off with **drug therapy**.

- The person could begin to feel like he or she is to **blame** for their problems.

Practice Questions

Q1 Outline Ellis's ABC model.

Q2 What three factors make up Beck's 'negative triad'?

Q3 What is the main aim of CBT?

Exam Questions

Q1 Outline the assumptions of the cognitive explanation of depression.   [4 marks]

Q2 Evaluate the cognitive explanation of depression.   [6 marks]

Q3 Outline and evaluate the cognitive approach to treating depression.   [12 marks]

I think, therefore I am. Depressed...

So that was the cognitive approach to depression. You need to know the explanation, the treatment, and the strengths and weaknesses of both. It's a wonder the psychologists who come up with these theories don't get more depressed themselves. You'd think having thousands of AS students saying their ideas are a bit weak might upset them slightly...

The Behavioural Approach to Phobias

There are various explanations for how phobias develop, and how to treat them, but you only need to learn the behavioural approach. Which is great — it's my favourite. Although I'm not too keen on the picture at the bottom of the next page...

The Behavioural Model of Abnormality says **Behaviours** are all **Learnt**

Behaviourists argue that **phobias** are learnt in the same way that all behaviours are learnt — through **classical** and **operant conditioning**.

The behavioural approach is covered in detail in Section Four.

Classical Conditioning

See page 43 for more on classical conditioning.

1) In **classical conditioning** a natural reflex is produced in response to a previously neutral stimulus — **phobias** can be created when the **natural fear** response becomes associated with a particular stimulus.

A certain stimulus, e.g. a loud noise (unconditioned stimulus — UCS)	triggers →	a natural reflex, e.g. fear (unconditioned response — UCR)
UCS repeatedly presented with another stimulus, e.g. a rat (conditioned stimulus — CS)	triggers →	fear (unconditioned response — UCR)
Over time, the rat presented by itself	triggers →	fear (conditioned response — CR)

2) Phobias can **generalise** to similar stimuli (see page 43). For example, **Watson and Rayner (1920)** conditioned a phobia in Little Albert using the method above (see page 45). Albert's resulting phobia of white rats was generalised to fluffy white objects.

Operant Conditioning

See page 44 for more on operant conditioning.

1) **Operant conditioning** is learning from the **consequences** of actions. Actions which have a good outcome through **positive reinforcement** (reward) or **negative reinforcement** (removal of something bad) will be repeated. Actions which have a bad outcome (**punishment**) will not be repeated.

2) Operant conditioning is important in **maintaining** phobias (see below).

The **Two-Process Model** Explains how **Phobias** are **Produced** and **Maintained**

Mowrer's **two-process model** (1947) explains how classical and operant conditioning produce and maintain phobias.

1) People develop phobias (usually specific phobias) by **classical conditioning** — a CS (conditioned stimulus) is paired with an UCS (unconditioned stimulus) to produce the CR (conditioned response).

2) Once somebody has developed a phobia, it's maintained through **operant conditioning** — people get anxious around the phobic stimulus and avoid it. This prevents the anxiety, which acts as **negative reinforcement**.

Operant conditioning can also explain how **social phobia** and **agoraphobia** develop from a specific phobia — people are anxious that they'll experience a **panic attack** in a social situation or an open place (because of their specific phobia), so they avoid these situations.

Social phobia or agoraphobia can develop on their own through classical conditioning (if the anxiety-inducing situations have been paired with an unconditioned stimulus).

The **Behavioural** Explanation of **Phobias** Has **Strengths** and **Weaknesses**

Strengths:

1) **Barlow and Durand (1995)** showed that in cases of individuals with a severe fear of driving, **50%** of them had actually been involved in a road accident. Through **classical conditioning**, the road accident (an UCS) had turned driving into a CS for those now with the phobia.

2) Behavioural **therapies** are very **effective** at treating phobias by getting the person to **change** their **response** to the **stimulus** (see next page). This suggests that they treat the **cause** of the problem.

Weakness:

1) **Davey (1992)** found that only **7%** of spider phobics recalled having a **traumatic experience** with a spider.

2) This suggests that there could be **other explanations**, e.g. biological factors. (But just because they couldn't remember the experience, this doesn't mean it didn't happen.)

The Behavioural Approach to Phobias

Phobias Can be Treated Using Behavioural Therapies

Behavioural treatment for **phobias** is based on **classical conditioning** — there are **two techniques**:

Systematic desensitisation

1) Systematic desensitisation works by using **counter-conditioning** so that the person learns to **associate** the **phobic stimulus** with **relaxation** rather than **fear**.

2) First, the phobic person makes a **'fear hierarchy'**. This is a list of feared events, showing what they fear least (e.g. seeing a picture of a spider) through to their most feared event (e.g. holding a spider).

3) They are then taught **relaxation techniques** like deep breathing.

4) The patient then **imagines** the anxiety-provoking situations, starting with the least stressful. They're encouraged to use the **relaxation techniques**, and the process stops if they feel anxious.

> Real-life situations can also be used (rather than just the imagination), for example actually looking at a spider.

5) Relaxation and anxiety can't happen at the same time, so when they become relaxed and calm, they're no longer scared. This is repeated until the feared event is only linked with **relaxation**.

6) This whole process is repeated for each stage of the fear hierarchy, until they are **calm** through their **most feared** event.

Flooding

1) This involves exposing the patient to the phobic stimulus **straight away**, without any relaxation or gradual build-up. This can be done in **real life**, or the patient can be asked to **visualise** it. For example, someone who was afraid of heights might imagine standing on top of a skyscraper.

2) The patient is kept in this situation until the **anxiety** they feel at first has **worn off**. They realise that nothing bad has happened to them in this time, and their fear should be **extinguished**.

Advantages

- **Behavioural therapy** is very effective for treating **specific phobias**. **Zinbarg et al (1992)** found that **systematic desensitisation** was the **most effective** of the currently known methods for treating phobias.

- It works very **quickly**, e.g. **Ost et al (1991)** found that anxiety was reduced in **90%** of patients with a specific phobia after just **one session** of **therapy**.

Disadvantages

- There are **ethical issues** surrounding behavioural therapy — especially **flooding**, as it causes patients a lot of anxiety. If patients **drop out** of the therapy **before** the fear has been extinguished, then it can end up causing **more anxiety** than before therapy started.

- **Behavioural therapy** only treats the **symptoms** of the disorder. **Other therapies** try to tackle the **cause** of it, e.g. cognitive behaviour therapy.

Practice Questions

Q1 How might a specific phobia develop through classical conditioning?

Q2 What is the behavioural therapy, flooding?

Q3 Give one strength of the behavioural approach to treating phobias.

Exam Questions

Q1 Outline systematic desensitisation as a treatment for phobias. [4 marks]

Q2 Outline and evaluate the behavioural explanation of phobias. [12 marks]

So, you're scared of spiders — oooh, look what I have here...

Hmmm... you wouldn't be able to use the excuse of 'phobia of revision' if your teacher was a behaviourist. So I guess you'd better just get on with it just in case. Doing well in your exam will be a positive reinforcement — or something...

The Biological Approach to OCD

There's more than one approach to explaining and treating OCD, but you just need to know about the biological one. Shame really — it's all interesting stuff. Ah well, can't win them all. Best just get stuck into this biological stuff. Read on...

The Biological Model Assumes Psychological Disorders are **Physical Illnesses**

The **biological approach** assumes that psychological disorders are **physical illnesses** with physical causes. In principle they're no different from physical illnesses like flu, except they have major psychological symptoms.

There are several **biological explanations** for **OCD**:

The biological approach is covered in detail in Section Four.

1) **Genetic** Factors

Some researchers think that **genetics** plays a part in OCD. Studies have looked at OCD rates among people with a relative who has OCD, to see if having a relative with OCD **significantly** increases your chances of developing it.

EVIDENCE FOR

1) **Billet et al (1998)** did a **meta-analysis** of twin studies that had been carried out over a long period of time. They found that for **identical twins**, if one twin had OCD then **68%** of the time both twins had it, compared to **31%** for **non-identical twins**.

2) **Pauls et al (2005)** found that **10%** of people with an **immediate relative** (i.e. parents, offspring or siblings) with OCD also suffered from the disorder. This is compared to around **2%** of people in the general population.

EVIDENCE AGAINST

1) No study has found a **100%** concordance rate, so **genetics can't** be the full story in OCD. It's possible that children **imitate** the obsessive and compulsive behaviour of their relatives.

2) Concordance rates don't prove that OCD is **caused** by genetics. It may be that **general anxiety** is genetic and that going on to develop OCD itself has **other contributing factors**, e.g. biochemical or psychological factors.

Concordance means how likely it is that both people in a pair will have a certain characteristic, given that one of them does.

2) **Biochemical** Factors

PET scans have shown that levels of the **neurotransmitter serotonin** are lower in OCD sufferers.

EVIDENCE FOR

1) **Insel (1991)** found that a class of drugs called **SSRIs**, which increase levels of serotonin, can reduce symptoms of OCD in **50 to 60%** of cases. There's more about this on the next page.

2) **Zohar et al (1996)** also found that **SSRIs alleviated symptoms** in **60%** of patients with OCD.

EVIDENCE AGAINST

1) SSRIs appear to offer some relief to sufferers of OCD. However, as this is **not** true in **100%** of cases, there must be **more** to understanding OCD.

2) The **link** with serotonin is **correlational**, so it doesn't show **cause and effect**. It may be that decreased serotonin levels are a **symptom** of OCD, rather than a cause of it.

3) **Neurological** Factors

Some research using **PET scans** has found that **abnormality** in the **basal ganglia** within the brain may be linked to OCD.

EVIDENCE FOR

1) **Max et al (1995)** found **increased rates** of OCD in people after **head injuries** that caused brain damage to the **basal ganglia**.

2) Other researchers have found **increased activity** in this area during OCD-related thoughts and behaviours.

3) OCD is often found in people with **other diseases** which involve the basal ganglia, e.g. **Parkinson's** and **Huntington's disease**.

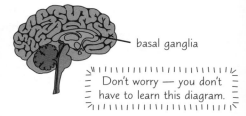

basal ganglia

Don't worry — you don't have to learn this diagram.

EVIDENCE AGAINST

1) **Aylward et al (1996)** didn't find a significant difference in **basal ganglia impairment** between OCD patients and controls.

2) Basal ganglia damage **hasn't** been found in **100%** of people with OCD, so it can't be the full story.

The Biological Approach to OCD

The **Biological** Explanation of **OCD** Has **Strengths** and **Weaknesses**

Strengths:

1) It has a **scientific** basis in biology — there's evidence that low serotonin and damage to the basal ganglia **correlate** with cases of OCD, though this doesn't necessarily show a **causal** relationship.

2) **Twin studies** have shown that genetics have at least some effect on the likelihood of developing OCD.

3) It can be seen as **ethical** — people **aren't blamed** for their disorders; they just have an illness.

Weaknesses:

1) The explanation doesn't take into account the effect of the **environment**, **family**, **childhood experiences** or **social influences** — psychologists taking other approaches consider these sorts of things important factors.

2) Biological therapies raise **ethical** concerns. Drugs can produce addiction and may only suppress symptoms rather than cure the disorder.

OCD Can be **Treated** Using **Biological Therapy**

1) The **biological** approach to treating OCD involves **drug therapy**.

2) Drug treatments usually work by increasing levels of **serotonin** in the brain using **selective serotonin reuptake inhibitors (SSRIs)**. These are a type of **antidepressant** drug that **increase** the availability of **serotonin**.

3) SSRIs **prevent the reuptake** of serotonin in the **synaptic cleft** (the gap between two neurons). This means there's **more serotonin** available to the next neuron.

Advantages

- Several researchers have found SSRIs to be **effective** in treating OCD. **Thoren et al** (1980) found that use of an SSRI was significantly better at **reducing obsessional thoughts** than a placebo.

- Research has found that using **other antidepressants** that don't affect serotonin levels is **ineffective** at reducing OCD symptoms.

OCD affects lots of people in the UK. If sufferers can have the most appropriate treatment, they can maintain a better quality of life and remain effective members of society.

Disadvantages

- Up to **50%** of patients with OCD **don't** experience any improvement in their symptoms when taking SSRIs. Out of those that do improve, up to **90%** have a **relapse** when they stop taking them.

- SSRIs have to be taken for **several weeks** before the patient experiences an improvement in their symptoms.

- **Side effects** of using these types of drugs include **nausea** and **headaches**, and sometimes increased levels of **anxiety**. This can cause people to **stop taking** their medication.

Practice Questions

Q1 What is the main idea behind the biological approach to explaining psychological disorders?
Q2 Outline a study that shows that OCD has a genetic factor.
Q3 Outline the link between serotonin levels and OCD.
Q4 Give one piece of evidence for the neurological explanation of OCD.
Q5 What are SSRIs?

Exam Questions

Q1 Briefly outline one weakness of the biological explanation of OCD. [2 marks]

Q2 Outline and evaluate the biological approach to treating OCD. [12 marks]

And there was me thinking basal ganglia was a sub-genre of reggae...

So there are several biological factors that might explain OCD, and there's evidence for and against all of them. Oh well. Make sure you've learnt them all, and you can evaluate each of them, as well as the biological explanation of OCD as a whole. You need to be able to explain and evaluate drug therapy for OCD too. Then you can have a little lie down...

Research Methods

This is everything you could ever want to know (and probably a bit more too...) about how psychologists go about testing their theories. Have a look at pages 91-93 for more on the ethical issues surrounding different research methods.

There are Several Types of **Experiment**

An **experiment** is a way of conducting research in a **controlled** way.
There are several types:

1) **Laboratory** Experiments

The aim of laboratory experiments is to **control** all relevant variables except for **one key variable**, which is altered to see what the effect is. The variable that you alter is called the **independent variable** (see page 79). Laboratory experiments are conducted in an **artificial setting**, e.g. Milgram's study (see page 7).

Strengths

Control — the effects of confounding variables (those that have an effect in addition to the variable of interest — see page 79) are minimised.

Replication — strict controls mean you can run the study again to check the findings.

Causal relationships — ideally it's possible to establish whether one variable actually causes change in another.

Limitations

Artificial — experiments might not measure real-life behaviour (i.e. they may lack ecological validity).

Demand characteristics — participants may respond according to what they think is being investigated, which can bias the results.

Ethics — deception is often used, making informed consent difficult.

2) **Field** Experiments

Field experiments are conducted **outside** the laboratory.
Behaviour is measured in a **natural environment** like a school, the street or on a train.
A **key variable** is still altered so that its effect can be measured.

> Laboratory and field experiments are 'true experiments' because variables can be controlled and manipulated.

Strengths

Causal relationships — you can still establish causal relationships by manipulating the key variable and measuring its effect, although it's very difficult to do in a field experiment.

Ecological validity — field experiments are less artificial than those done in a laboratory, so they relate to real life better.

Demand characteristics (participants trying to guess what the researcher expects from them and performing differently because of it) — these can be avoided if participants don't know they're in a study.

Pierre was quite a pro at carrying out field experiments.

Limitations

Less control — confounding variables may be more likely in a natural environment.

Ethics — participants who didn't agree to take part might experience distress and often can't be debriefed. Observation must respect privacy.

Research Methods

3) *Natural* Experiments

This is where the researcher looks at how an **independent variable**, which **isn't manipulated** by the researchers, affects a **dependent variable**. The independent variable isn't manipulated because it's an **event** which occurs **naturally**. An **example** is research into the **effect** of a single-sex school and a mixed-sex school on **behaviour**. Participants are usually allocated to conditions **randomly**.

Strengths

Ethical — it's possible to study variables that it would be unethical to manipulate, e.g. you can compare a community that has TV with a community that doesn't to see which is more aggressive.

Demand characteristics — participants might not know they're in a study, so their behaviour is likely to be more natural.

Ecological validity — they tend to be less artificial than laboratory experiments.

Limitations

Causal relationships — because you don't manipulate the independent variable, and because other variables could be having an effect, it's hard to establish causal relationships.

Ethics — deception is often used, making informed consent difficult.
Also, confidentiality may be compromised if the community is identifiable.

4) *Quasi* Experiments

In a **quasi experiment**, the researcher **isn't** able to use **random allocation** to put participants in different conditions. This is usually because the **independent variable** is a particular **feature** of the participants, such as **gender** or the existence of a **mental disorder**.

Strengths

Control — quasi experiments are often carried out under controlled conditions.

Ecological validity — the research is often less artificial than laboratory studies, so you're more likely to be able to generalise the results to real life.

Limitations

Participant allocation — you can't randomly allocate participants to each condition, and so confounding variables (e.g. what area the participants live in) may affect results. Let's face it — you've got no control over these variables, so it's ridiculously hard to say what's caused by what.

Causal relationships — it can be hard to establish cause and effect because the independent variable isn't being directly manipulated.

Practice Questions

Q1 What are the main strengths of laboratory experiments?

Q2 Outline one limitation of field experiments.

Q3 What is a quasi experiment?

Exam Questions

Q1	Outline one limitation of a laboratory experiment.	[2 marks]
Q2	Outline one strength of a field experiment.	[2 marks]
Q3	Outline **two** limitations of natural experiments.	[4 marks]

It's only natural to feel a bit quasi at this point in time...

This is one hefty section on research methods, so it's understandable that you may feel a bit daunted by it all. But fear not — all will be fine. I promise. Once you've mastered these pages on experimental methods, you can move on to observational, self-report and correlation methods. You'll be experimenting on people in no time*...

*as long as it's done ethically, please.

Research Methods

And yes, there are more...

Observational Techniques Involve Observing — NOT Interfering

Naturalistic observation involves observing subjects in their natural environment. Researchers take great care not to interfere in any way with the subjects they're studying.

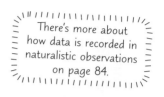

There's more about how data is recorded in naturalistic observations on page 84.

Strengths

Ecological validity — the participants' behaviour is natural and there are no demand characteristics, as the participant is unaware of being observed.

Theory development — these studies can be a useful way of developing ideas about behaviour that could be tested in more controlled conditions later.

Limitations

Extraneous variables — you can't control variables that may affect behaviour.

Observer bias — the observers' expectations may affect what they focus on and record. This means the reliability of the results may be a problem — another observer may have come up with very different results.

Ethics — you should only conduct observations where people might expect to be observed by strangers. This limits the situations where you can do a naturalistic observation. Debriefing is difficult. Observation must respect privacy. Getting informed consent can be tricky.

Another type of observation is **controlled observation**. This is where the situation is carried out in conditions set up by the researcher. Although the variables are **more controlled**, these studies have **lower** ecological validity and participants may behave **differently** if they know they're being observed.

Correlational Research Looks for Relationships Between Variables

Correlational research looks for a **relationship** between **two variables**. As these variables **aren't manipulated** as in an experiment, it's not possible to state that **just** these two variables rise and fall together, or that one variable is **causing** the change in the other — the pattern may be the result of a third **unknown variable** or be just a **coincidence**.

Strengths

Causal relationships — these can be ruled out if no correlation exists.

Ethics — you can study variables that it would be unethical to manipulate, e.g. is there a relationship between the number of cigarettes smoked and incidences of ill health?

Limitations

Causal relationships — these cannot be assumed from a correlation, which may be caused by a third, unknown variable.

Ethics — misinterpretation can be an issue. Sometimes the media (and researchers) infer causality from a correlation.

Self-Report Techniques Involve Questionnaires and Interviews

1) Questionnaires Can be Written, Face-to-Face, on the Phone or Via the Internet

Strengths | **Practical** — you can collect a large amount of information quickly and relatively cheaply.

Limitations

Bad questions — leading questions (questions that suggest answers) or unclear questions can be a problem.

Biased samples — some people are more likely to respond, making a sample unrepresentative.

Self-report — people often wish to present themselves in a good light (social desirability bias — see p.89). What they say and what they actually think could be different, making any results unreliable.

Ethics — confidentiality can be a problem, especially around sensitive issues.

Research Methods

2) *Interviews* are More Like a *Conversation* than a Face-to-Face Questionnaire

Structured interviews follow a fixed set of questions that are the same for all participants.
Unstructured interviews may have a set of discussion topics, but are less constrained about how the conversation goes.

Strengths

Rich data — you can get detailed information, as there are fewer constraints than with a questionnaire. Unstructured interviews provide richer information than structured interviews.

Pilot study — interviews are a useful way to get information before a study.

Limitations

Self-report — the results can be unreliable and affected by social desirability bias (see questionnaires).

Impractical — conducting interviews can be time-consuming and requires skilled researchers.

Data analysis — analysing the data can be hard, particularly for unstructured interviews, because there could be a huge amount of qualitative data, which can be tricky to analyse (see page 87).

Ethics — confidentiality can be a problem, especially around sensitive issues.

Case Studies are Intensive *Descriptions* of a *Single* Individual or Case

Case studies allow researchers to analyse unusual cases in a lot of detail, e.g. Milner et al's study of **HM** (page 17).

Strengths

Rich data — researchers have the opportunity to study rare phenomena in a lot of detail.

Unique cases — can challenge existing ideas and theories, and suggest ideas for future research.

Limitations

Causal relationships — cause-and-effect of a relationship cannot be established.

Generalisation — only studying a single case makes generalising the results extremely difficult.

Ethics — informed consent can be difficult to obtain in some cases.

Practice Questions

Q1 Give one strength of naturalistic observations.

Q2 What does correlational research look for?

Q3 How can questionnaires be distributed?

Q4 Write down one limitation of collecting data using questionnaires.

Q5 What is the difference between a structured interview and an unstructured interview.

Exam Questions

Q1 Outline one limitation of collecting data using naturalistic observation. [1 mark]

Q2 Keenan used a correlational study to investigate the relationship between participants' caffeine consumption and their scores on a Psychology exam.
Describe one strength and one limitation of Keenan's choice of research method. [2 marks]

Q3 Which of the following do not involve self-report techniques?

    A structured interviews   **B** observations   **C** unstructured interviews   **D** questionnaires   [1 mark]

Big Brother — naturalistic observation at its finest...?

When you're carrying out an observation, you want to see behaviour that's as natural as possible. What you don't want is for people to put on an act just because they're aware that they're being watched — that defeats the object of doing the study in the first place. Makes you wonder about Big Brother — do we actually get to see some natural stuff?

Aims and Hypotheses

When research is conducted, the idea is to carry out an objective test of something, i.e. to obtain a scientific measurement of how people behave — not just someone's opinion. Well that's what I reckon...

Research Aims are Important

An **aim** is a statement of a study's purpose — for example, Asch's aim might have been: 'To study majority influence in an unambiguous task'. (See page 3 for the details of Asch's study.)

Research should state its aim **beforehand** so that it's **clear** what the study intends to investigate.

Hypotheses are Theories Tested by Research

Although the **aim** states the **purpose** of a study, it isn't usually **precise** enough to **test**. What is needed are clear statements of what's actually being tested — the **hypotheses**. A hypothesis is worded in a way that states a **prediction** of what will be shown by the research.

1) **NULL HYPOTHESIS**

The **null hypothesis** is what you're going to **assume is true** during the study. Any data you collect will either back this assumption up, or it won't. If the data **doesn't support** your null hypothesis, you **reject** it and go with your **alternative hypothesis** instead.

Very often, the null hypothesis is a prediction that there will be **no relationship** between the key variables in a study (and any correlation is due to **chance**), or that there will be **no difference** between the scores from the various conditions of an experiment. (An example might be that there will be no significant difference in exam grades between students who use a revision guide and students who don't.)

(Note: It's quite usual to have something you **don't actually believe** as your null hypothesis. You assume it **is** true for the duration of the study, then if your results lead you to reject this null hypothesis, you've **proved** it **wasn't true** after all.)

2) **ALTERNATIVE HYPOTHESIS**

If the data forces you to **reject** your null hypothesis, then you accept your **alternative hypothesis** instead.

So if your null hypothesis was that two variables **aren't** linked, then your alternative hypothesis would be that they **are** linked. Or you can be more specific, and be a bit more precise about **how** they are linked, using **directional** hypotheses (see below).

3) **DIRECTIONAL HYPOTHESIS**

A hypothesis might predict a difference between the exam results obtained by two groups of students — a group that uses a revision guide and another group that doesn't.

If the hypothesis states which group will do better, it is making a **directional prediction**.

For example, you might say that students who use a revision guide will get **significantly higher** exam grades than students who don't — this is a directional hypothesis.

Directional hypotheses are often used when **previous research findings** suggest which way the results will go.

4) **NON-DIRECTIONAL HYPOTHESIS**

A **non-directional hypothesis** would predict a difference, but wouldn't say which group would do better.

For example, you might just say that there will be a **significant difference** in exam grades between students who use a revision guide and students who don't — this is a **non-directional** hypothesis, since you're not saying which group will do better.

Non-directional hypotheses can be used when there is **little previous research** in the area under investigation, or when previous research findings are **mixed** and **inconclusive**.

Aims and Hypotheses

Some *Variables* are *Manipulated* by the Researcher — Others Aren't

A **variable** is a quantity whose **value** can **change** — for example, the time taken to do a task, someone's anxiety level, or an exam result. In an experiment, there are various different kinds of variable.

The **Independent Variable** is **Directly** Manipulated

1) An **independent variable (IV)** is a variable **directly manipulated** by the researcher.

2) In the example on the previous page about students, exams and revision guides, there are two variables. One is 'whether or not a revision guide is used' (so this variable has only two possible values: yes and no). The other is the 'exam grade' (and this could have lots of possible values: e.g. A, B, C, D, E, U).

3) In this case, the **independent variable** is 'whether or not a revision guide is used' — since this is **directly** under the control of the researcher.

The **Dependent Variable** is Only Affected **Indirectly**

1) The **dependent variable (DV)** is the variable that you think will be **affected** by changes in the independent variable. (So the DV is **dependent on** the **IV**.)

2) In the exam grades example, the dependent variable is the 'exam grade'. The exam grade is dependent on whether a revision guide was used (or at least, that's what's being **investigated**).

Ideally in a study the *only* thing that would influence the **DV** (the thing you're measuring) would be the **IV** (the thing you're manipulating). Usually though, there are other things that will have an effect.

An **extraneous variable** is any variable (other than the **IV**) that **could** affect what you're trying to measure. If these things **are** actually **influencing** the DV then they're called **confounding variables**.

Operationalisation *is* *Showing* How the Variables Will Be *Measured*

1) Variables must be **operationalised**. This means describing the **process** by which the variable is **measured**.

2) Some things are easy to operationalise (e.g. **height** might be operationalised as 'the distance in centimetres from the bottom of an object to the top'). Other things are difficult to operationalise (e.g. a mother's love for her newborn baby).

3) **Operationalisation** allows others to see exactly how you're going to define and measure your variables. It also has 18 letters, which is the same as soporiferousnesses, or yaaaaaaawwwwwwwwwwn.

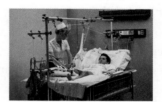

"Don't worry, sir — once we get your variable operationalised you'll be right as rain."

Practice Questions

Q1 When would you reject the null hypothesis?

Q2 What is the difference between a directional and a non-directional hypothesis?

Q3 What is an independent variable?

Exam Question

Q1 Eva is interested in whether taking fish oil supplements every day for a month can improve memory performance.

  a) Identify the independent variable in Eva's study. [1 mark]

  b) What would be an appropriate hypothesis for her study? [3 marks]

Aim to learn this page — I hypothesise you'll need it...

Remember, you assume the null hypothesis is true unless your data suggests otherwise — if it does then you quickly switch allegiance to the alternative hypothesis instead. And remember, the IV is deliberately manipulated by the researcher. This might lead to an effect on the DV, but it's often a kind of indirect, knock-on effect. That's enough now.

Experimental Design

Once you've got a theory, this is how you'd actually go about researching it...

The **Experimental Design** Must Make the Hypothesis **Testable**

> **Research example** — does the presence of an audience help or hinder people doing the 'wiggly wire' task (moving a loop along a wire without touching it and setting off the buzzer)?
>
> Based on previous research, we expect people to do this better without anyone watching them.

1) The **IV** (the variable being manipulated) is the presence or absence of an audience.

2) The **DV** (the variable being measured) is 'how well' the participants do on the task — but it must be testable. You need a **precisely defined** (or **operationalised**) DV, which should be **quantitative** wherever possible. An operationalised DV for this experiment might be 'the time taken to move the loop from one end of the wire to the other without setting off the buzzer'.

There are Three **Experimental Designs** that are Used Loads

1) An **independent groups design** means there are **different participants** in each group. Here, for example, one group does the task **with** an audience and another group does it **alone**.

   This avoids the problem that if all the participants did the test in both conditions, any improvement in performance might be due to them having two goes at the task (which would be a confounding variable).

Advantages	**Disadvantages**
No **order effects** — no one gets better through practice (**learning effect**) or gets worse through being bored or tired (**fatigue effect**).	**Participant variables** — differences between the **people** in each group might affect the results (e.g. the 'without audience' group may just have people who are better at the task — so we can't safely compare groups).
	Number of participants — **twice as many** participants are needed to get the same amount of data, compared to having everyone do both conditions.

2) A **repeated measures design** is where, e.g., all participants do the task both **with** an audience and then **without**. You can compare the performances in each condition knowing the differences weren't due to participant variables.

Advantages	**Disadvantages**
Participant variables — now the same people do the test in both conditions, so any differences between individuals shouldn't affect the results.	**Order effects** — if all participants did the 'with audience' condition first, any improvements in the second condition could be due to **practice**, not the audience's absence. (But see **counterbalancing** on the next page.)
Number of participants — **fewer** participants are needed to get the same amount of data.	

3) A **matched pairs design** means there are different participants in each condition, but they're **matched** on important variables (like age, sex and personality). For example, the participants are paired on a relevant characteristic, such as age, and then the two members of the pair are **randomly assigned** to **either** the 'audience' or 'no audience' condition to ensure that **each condition** has a **similar age range**.

Advantages	**Disadvantages**
No **order effects** — there are **different people** in each condition.	**Number of participants** — need twice as many people compared to repeated measures.
Participant variables — important differences are minimised through **matching**.	**Practicalities** — **time-consuming** and difficult to find participants who **match**.

Some studies use **control groups**. These groups have not experienced any of the manipulations of the **IV** that an experimental group might have. This allows the researcher to make a direct comparison between them.

Experimental Design

It's Sometimes Good to Run a Small *Pilot Study* First

1) No piece of research is perfect. To help foresee any problems, a small-scale **pilot study** can be run first.

2) This should establish whether the **design** works, whether **participants** understand the wording in **instructions**, or whether something important has been **missed out**.

3) Problems can be tackled before running the **main study**, which could save wasting a lot of **time** and **money**.

Research Should Be Highly *Controlled*

1) Research needs to be highly **controlled** to avoid the effects of **extraneous variables** (see page 79).

2) Extraneous variables can be **controlled** in a study so that they're **kept constant** for all participants. For example, everyone could do the task in the same place so distractions are similar.

3) Extraneous variables can also be **eliminated altogether**. For example, everyone could do the task somewhere with no noise distractions — shhhh...

4) There are lots of other ways that research can be controlled to eliminate extraneous variables:

Counterbalancing

- **Counterbalancing** (mixing up the order of the tasks) can solve **order effects** in **repeated measures** designs.
- Half the participants do the task **with** an audience **first** and **then without**. The others do the conditions **the other way round**. Any order effects would then be equal across conditions and so will cancel each other out.

Random Allocation

- **Random allocation** (e.g. by drawing names out of a hat) means everyone has an **equal chance** of doing **either** condition.
- An **independent measures** study with, for example, more men in one group than the other could have a confounding variable (see page 79). Any difference in performance may be due to **sex** rather than the real IV.
- Random allocation should ensure groups are **not biased** on key variables.

Ralph thought doing his experiment on a desert island would eliminate extraneous variables. He hadn't anticipated the seals.

Standardised Instructions

- **Standardised instructions** should ensure the **experimenters** act in a similar way with all participants.
- Everything should be **as similar as possible** for all the participants, including each participant's **experience** in such studies.

Randomisation

- **Randomisation** is when the **material** is presented to the participants in a random order. It avoids the possibility of **order effects**.
- For example, in a **repeated measures** memory experiment, participants may be asked to learn a list of words in two different conditions. In each condition, the words on their lists would be in a **random** order.

Experimental Design

Researchers have to Consider **Reliability** and **Validity**

Reliability

- If a test is consistent within itself, it has **internal reliability**. The **split-half technique** assesses this. A questionnaire is randomly split in two — if all participants score similarly on both halves, the questions measure the same thing.
- If the measure is stable over time or between people, then it has **external reliability**. This can be assessed by measuring **test-retest reliability** (does the same person always score similarly on the test?) or **inter-rater reliability** (do different assessors agree, i.e. do they both give the same score?).

Validity

- If an experiment shows that the results were caused by the manipulation of the **variables**, rather than the effect of something else, then it has **internal validity**.
- If the findings can be **generalised** beyond the experimental setting (e.g. to different groups of people or different settings), then the experiment has **external validity**.
- **Ecological validity** is the measure of how true the results are to real life. So if something has **high** ecological validity, it means that the results are representative of what would happen in the real world. Lab studies have **low ecological validity** because they're artificial and so it's harder to generalise the results to the wider population.

Practice Questions

Q1 Give one disadvantage of an independent groups design.

Q2 Give one design that overcomes the disadvantage you identified in Q1.

Q3 What are the main benefits of running a pilot study?

Q4 Define 'ecological validity'.

Exam Question

Q1 Read the information below and then answer the questions that follow.

> A psychologist wanted to investigate the effect of exercise on memory. She used **two** conditions:
>
> **Condition A**: Participants were asked to learn a list of 30 words, run on a treadmill for 10 minutes at a standardised speed, and then recall as many words as they could.
>
> **Condition B**: Participants were asked to learn a list of 30 words, wait for 10 minutes in silence, and then recall as many words as they could.
>
> 40 participants were used in total. Half took part in Condition A, followed by Condition B, and the other half did Condition B, followed by Condition A.

a) Name the experimental design used in this study. [1 mark]

b) What technique has the psychologist used to reduce order effects? [1 mark]

c) Outline how this experiment could be altered to use a different experimental design. [3 marks]

Inter-test validity, no... split-rater ethics, no... oh pants... zzzzzzzzz...

There are lots of details here, but they're all really important. If you're not really careful when you design a piece of research, the results you get might not be worth the paper you end up writing them down on. And that'd be no good. Spending a little bit of time thinking at the design stage will make it all worth it in the end — trust me.

Observations, Questionnaires and Interviews

These pages will tell you everything you could ever wish to know about observations, questionnaires and interviews. Bit of a jam-packed few pages, eh? Best get reading...

Researchers Can use Participant or Non-Participant Observation

1) **Participant observation** is when the researcher **participates** in the activity under study.

   Advantages: — The researcher develops a relationship with the group under study, so they can gain a greater understanding of the group's behaviour.

   Disadvantages: — The researcher loses objectivity by becoming part of the group.
   — The participants may act differently if they know a researcher is amongst them.

2) **Non-participant observation** is when the researcher observes the activity without getting involved in it.

   Advantages: — The researcher can remain objective throughout the study.

   Disadvantages: — The researcher loses a sense of the group dynamics by staying separate from the group.

   > Sometimes researchers undertake **structured observations**.
   > This is where the behaviour categories that are going to be used are defined in **advance**.
   > There's more on this on the next page.
   >
   > Advantages: — It's easier to gather relevant data because you already know what you're looking for.
   >
   > Disadvantages: — Interesting behaviours could go unrecorded because they haven't been pre-defined as important.

Participant and Non-Participant Observations Can be Overt or Covert

Participant and non-participant observations can either be:

Overt Observations

Overt observations are where the researcher's presence is **obvious** to the participants.

   Advantage: — They are much more ethically sound than other methods because the participants are aware of the research.

   Disadvantage: — People might change their behaviour if they know they're being observed.

Covert Observations

Covert observations are where the researcher's presence is **unknown** to the participants.

   Advantage: — The participants are much more likely to behave naturally.

   Disadvantage: — Gaining ethical approval may be difficult.

Arthur brought out his matching tracksuit to carry out his covert observation.

Controlled Observations have Conditions Set Up by the Experimenter

Controlled observations often take place in a laboratory so the researcher can control the conditions. Bandura's **Bobo doll study** (page 47) is an example of this type of observation.

   Advantages: — Because the study is highly controlled, it is possible to replicate it to check that the results are reliable.
   — A controlled environment means that extraneous variables can be controlled, so it becomes possible for cause and effect to be established.

   Disadvantages: — They will have lower ecological validity than naturalistic observations.
   — Participants may alter their behaviour if they know they're being observed.

Observations, Questionnaires and Interviews

Naturalistic Observation Involves Making Design Decisions

Naturalistic observations take place in a natural environment, rather than a lab.
They can be structured in advance to make sure no behaviours are missed.

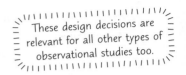

These design decisions are relevant for all other types of observational studies too.

Recording Data

If you want **qualitative data** you could just make **written notes**. But **video**
or **audio recording** means that you have a more accurate permanent record.

Categorising Behaviour

You must **define** the behaviours you aim to observe. For example, if you were going to observe children
in a school playground to see how many behave aggressively, you'd have to decide **what counts as
aggression**. This involves giving an **operationalised definition** (i.e. some **specific, observable** behaviours).

For example, you might say that *'aggression is any physical act made with
the intention to harm another person — such as punching, kicking, etc.'*

But you have to be careful not to **miss out** anything important otherwise your definition may not
be valid, e.g. aggression can also be verbal.

Rating Behaviour

The behaviours that you're interested in may be things that are a matter of **degree**, so you might
need to use a rating scale to classify behaviour.

You could put each participant's behaviour into one of several **categories**, e.g. *not aggressive,
mildly aggressive* or *very aggressive*.

Or you could use a **coding system** where each participant is given a **number** (e.g. between
1 and 10) to represent how aggressive they are, where a **higher score** indicates **more aggression**.

However, you still have to **define** what kinds of behaviour are included for each number on the
scale (e.g. 5 = *pushing* and 10 = *kicking or punching more than once*).
Behaviour rated in this way provides **quantitative data** (data in the form of **numbers**).

Sampling Behaviour

You have to decide **how often** and for **how long** you're going to observe the participants.

Event sampling — this is when you only record particular events that you're interested in
(e.g. aggression shown by the children) and ignore other behaviours.

    <u>Advantage</u> — Researchers know exactly what behaviours they're looking for.

    <u>Disadvantage</u> — Potentially interesting behaviours could be ignored.

Time-interval sampling — if the behaviours occur over a long time period you might choose
to observe for only set time intervals, e.g. the first 10 minutes of every hour. The time intervals
could be chosen randomly.

    <u>Advantage</u> — Very convenient for the researchers to carry out.

    <u>Disadvantage</u> — If interesting behaviours occur outside the sample intervals they won't be recorded.

Inter-Observer Reliability

Even after you've **defined** the behaviours you're interested in, you have to make sure that the
observers are actually putting each participant in the **right category** or giving the **right rating**.

This might involve **comparing** the data from two or more observers to make sure they're giving
the **same** scores (i.e. that they are 'reliable').

Observations, Questionnaires and Interviews

Questionnaires Need to be Designed Carefully

There are various things you need to consider when designing a questionnaire for a survey.

1) **Type of data** — whether you want **qualitative data** and/or **quantitative data** will affect whether you ask **open** and/or **closed questions**.

   a) **Open questions** are questions such as *What kinds of music do you like?*
   The participant can reply in **any way**, and in as much detail as they want. This gives detailed, qualitative information, although it may be **hard to analyse**, as the participants could give very different answers.

   b) **Closed questions** limit the answers that can be given, e.g. *Which do you like: Pop, Rock or neither?*
   They give **quantitative** data that is relatively **easy to analyse** — e.g. you can say exactly **how many** people liked each type of music. However, less detail is obtained about each participant.

2) **Ambiguity** — you have to avoid questions and answer options which are **not** clearly **defined**, e.g. *Do you listen to music frequently?* What is meant here by 'frequently' — once a day, once a week?

3) **Double-barrelled questions** — it's best not to use these, since a person may wish to answer **differently** to each part. For example, *Do you agree that modern music is not as good as the music of the 1960s and that there should be more guitar-based music in the charts?*

4) **Leading questions** — these are questions that **lead** the participant towards a particular answer. E.g. *How old was the boy in the distance?* They might have seen an older person, but by saying '*boy*' you're leading them to describe the person as young. You're also leading them to think that the person was male, but they might not have been sure. (It's really important to avoid leading questions in **eyewitness testimony** — see p.22-25.)

5) **Complexity** — whenever possible, **clear English** should be used, avoiding **jargon**.
   However, if specialist terms are included, they should be clearly defined.
   (So the question *Do you prefer music written in unusual time signatures?* probably isn't ideal for most people.)

All of the Above Goes for Interviews As Well

But you also have to consider the following:

1) **How structured** the interview will be:
   Interviews can be very **informal** with **few set questions**, and new questions being asked **depending on** the participant's **previous answers**. This gives detailed qualitative data, which may be difficult to analyse. Alternatively, they may be more **structured**, with set questions and **closed answers**, giving **less detail** but being **easier to analyse**.

2) Using a **question checklist** — if the interview is structured, a checklist ensures that no questions are left out and questions aren't asked twice.

3) The behaviour or appearance of the **interviewer** — this could **influence** how the participants react.

Practice Questions

Q1 What is 'non-participant observation'?
Q2 Give two advantages of using controlled observation.
Q3 Why is it important to define behavioural categories in naturalistic observations?
Q4 Outline three considerations involved in designing questionnaires.

Exam Questions

Q1 Outline how event sampling can be used as part of an observational research method. [2 marks]

Q2 Briefly outline **two** issues that a researcher must consider when conducting an interview. [4 marks]

I've always wanted to be an undercover cop...

Covert and participant observations sound like fun. It'd be a bit like being in one of those exciting crime TV programmes, where a policeman dresses up as a 'normal' person, gets involved in a high-speed car chase and saves the day by catching the criminal in his tracks. What I'd give to lead an exciting life. Oh, wait. I have Psychology. Yay.

Data Analysis

Data analysis might sound vaguely maths-like — but don't run for the hills just yet. It isn't too tricky...

Data from **Observations** Should be Analysed **Carefully**

1) If you've got **quantitative** data (i.e. numbers), you can use **statistics** to show, for example, the most common behaviours. Quantitative data can be obtained by **categorising** and **rating** behaviour — see page 84.

2) **Qualitative** data might consist of a video or audio **recording**, or written **notes** on what the observers witnessed. Analysis of qualitative data is **less straightforward**, but it can still be done.

3) Whatever kind of data you've got, there are some important issues to bear in mind:

   a) There must be **adequate data sampling** (see page 84) to ensure that a **representative** sample of participants' behaviour has been seen.

   b) **Language** must be used **accurately** — the words used to describe behaviour should be **accurate** and **appropriate** (and must have valid **operationalised definitions** — see page 84). For example, it might not be appropriate to describe a child's behaviour as 'aggressive' if he or she is play-fighting.

   c) Researcher **bias** must be **avoided** — e.g. it's not okay to make notes **only** on events that **support** the researcher's theories, or to have a **biased interpretation** of what is observed.

The Same Goes for Data Obtained from **Interviews**

1) When **closed** questions are used as part of an interview's structure, **quantitative** data can be produced (e.g. the **number** of participants who replied 'Yes' to a particular question). **Statistics** can then be used (see p.96-98 and p.104-105) to further analyse the data.

2) When **open** questions are used, more **detailed**, **qualitative** data is obtained.

3) Again, whatever you've got, there are certain things you'll need to remember:

   a) **Context** — the **situation** in which a participant says something, and the way they are **behaving** at the time, may be important. It may help the researcher understand **why** something is said, and give clues about the **honesty** of a statement.

   b) The researcher should clearly distinguish **what** is said by the participant from **how** they interpret it.

   c) **Selection** of data — a lot of **qualitative** data may be produced by an interview, which may be difficult for the researcher to **summarise** in a report. The researcher must **avoid bias** in selecting what to include (e.g. only including statements that support their ideas). The interviewees may be consulted when deciding **what** to include and **how** to present it.

   d) The interviewer should be aware of how *their* feelings about the interviewee could lead to **biased interpretations** of what they say, or how it is later reported.

And Likewise for Data from **Questionnaires**

1) Like observations and interviews, **questionnaires** can give you both **quantitative** and **qualitative** data, and so most of the points above are relevant to surveys as well.

2) Again, it's especially important to distinguish the **interpretations** of the **researcher** from the **statements** of the **participant**, and to be **unbiased** in selecting what to include in any report on the research.

3) However, the analysis of **written** answers may be especially difficult because the participant is not present to **clarify** any **ambiguities**, plus you don't know the **context** for their answers (e.g. what mood they were in, and so on).

Data Analysis

Qualitative Data Can be Tricky to Analyse

Qualitative data is sometimes seen as 'of **limited use**' because it's difficult to **analyse**.

1) Because of the **detail** (and hence the **insight**) that **qualitative** data can give, some researchers prefer to **avoid** 'reducing' it to **numbers**.

2) Instead they analyse the data into **categories** or '**typologies**' (e.g. sarcastic remarks, statements about feelings, etc.), **quotations**, **summaries**, and so on.

3) This is called **content analysis**.

4) **Hypotheses** may be developed during this analysis, rather than being stated previously, so that they are 'grounded in the data'.

Bertha was disappointed to learn that she'd been reduced to a number.

Summarising Lots of Studies is Called a Meta-Analysis

Both **quantitative** data and **qualitative** data can be analysed using a **meta-analysis**. This is where you analyse the results from loads of different studies and come up with some **general conclusions**.

They're a good way of **bringing together data** (which is a general aim of the scientific process), and by doing this they reduce the problem of **sample size**. However, one problem is that there are often loads of **conflicting results** out there, which obviously makes doing a meta-analysis a bit tricky...

Psychologists Gather Primary and Secondary Data

Researchers gather **primary** and **secondary data** when they collect results.

- **Primary data** — information collected during a researcher's direct observations of participants, e.g. test results, answers to questionnaires, observation notes.

- **Secondary data** — information collected from other studies. This data can be used to check the validity of studies, or used to provide evidence to support or discredit a new theory.

Practice Questions

Q1 What is quantitative data?
Q2 In what ways could a researcher be biased when analysing data from observations?
Q3 What type of questions will lead to detailed, qualitative data?
Q4 What is the difference between primary and secondary data?

Exam Questions

Q1 Collecting data on which of the following would produce qualitative data?
   A shoe size   **B** age   **C** opinions on car park charges   **D** time spent online each day   [1 mark]

Q2 Outline the main differences between qualitative and quantitative data-collection techniques.   [4 marks]

You must keep an open mind — but just don't let all the facts escape...

It's fairly obvious-ish, I guess, that qualitative data needs to be analysed with an open mind — it's not OK to fit the facts to your theory... you have to fit your theory to the facts. The same goes for analysing quantitative data — it's not just a case of 'doing some maths' — you have to be sure you're not being biased in your interpretations.

Selecting and Using Participants

It'd be great if you could study everyone in the world. It might take ages, but you're bound to find something interesting eventually. Most psychologists can't be bothered to do this though, so they just pick a selection of people to study...

Selecting a **Sample** of Participants Should be Done **Carefully**

1) The part of a **population** that you're interested in studying is called the **target group** — e.g. all the people in a particular city, or all people of a certain age or background.

2) Usually you can't include everyone in the target group in a study, so you choose a certain **sample** of **participants**.

3) This sample should be **representative** (i.e. it should reflect the variety of characteristics that are found in the target group) so that the results can be generalised to the whole target group.

4) A sample that is unrepresentative is **biased** and **can't** reliably be **generalised** to the whole target group.

There are five main ways of selecting a sample:

Random Sampling

This is when **every** member of the target group has an **equal chance** of being selected for the sample. This could be done either **manually** or by a **computer**. Manually, each person could be assigned a number. Each number could be put in a hat, and then numbers selected at random from it. Using a computer, everyone in the target group could be given a number, then the computer could randomly pick numbers to select participants. Sounds like being in a catalogue store. Order number 103 to the collection point...

Advantages: Random sampling is 'fair'. Everyone has an equal chance of being selected and the sample is **likely** to be representative.

Disadvantages: This method doesn't **guarantee** a representative sample — there's still a chance that some subgroups in the target group may not be selected (e.g. people from a minority cultural group). Also, if the target group is large it may not be practical (or possible) to give everyone a number that might be picked. So in practice, completely random samples are rarely used.

Opportunity Sampling

This is when the researcher samples whoever is **available and willing** to be studied. Since many researchers work in universities, they often use opportunity samples made up of students.

Advantages: This is a **quick** and **practical** way of getting a sample.

Disadvantages: The sample is **unlikely** to be **representative** of the target group or population as a whole. This means that we can't confidently **generalise** the findings of the research. However, because it's **quick** and **easy**, opportunity sampling is **often used**.

Volunteer Sampling

This is when people actively **volunteer** to be in a study by responding to a request for participants advertised by the researcher, e.g. in a newspaper or on a noticeboard.
The researcher may then select only those who are **suitable** for the study.
(This method was used by Milgram — see page 7.)

Advantages: If an advert is placed prominently (e.g. in a national newspaper) a **large number** of people may respond, giving more participants to study. This may allow more **in-depth analysis** and **more accurate** statistical results.

Disadvantages: Even though a large number of people may respond, these will only include people who saw or heard about the advertisement — no one else would have a chance of being selected. Also, people who volunteer may be more **cooperative** than others, so the sample is **unlikely** to be **representative** of the target population.

Selecting and Using Participants

Systematic Sampling

This is where every *n*th name from a **sampling frame** (a record of all the names in a population) is taken, e.g. every 3rd name from a register, or every 50th name from a phone book. This is useful if there is a sampling frame available.

Annie was promised systematic sampling was simple. Even her granny could do it.

Advantages: This is a **simple** and **effective** way of generating a sample with a random element. It also means that the population is more likely to be **evenly sampled** than by using opportunity or volunteer samples.

Disadvantages: Subgroups might be **missed**. It will not be **representative** if the pattern used for the **samples** coincides with a pattern in the **population**.

Stratified Sampling

This is where all of the **important subgroups** in the population (e.g. different age or ethnic groups) are identified and a proportionate number of each is randomly obtained. For example, in a class of **20** students, **ten** are 16 years old, **eight** are 17 years old and **two** are 18 years old. If you take a stratified sample of 10 students, the number of 16-, 17- and 18-year-olds in the sample will need to be **50%** of the full class. So you'll need **five** 16-year-olds, **four** 17-year-olds and **one** 18-year-old in your stratified sample.

Advantages: This can produce a fairly **representative** sample. It can also be used with random and systematic sampling.

Disadvantages: It can take a lot of **time** and **money** to do it, and some subgroups may be **missed**. It can often be **difficult** to identify traits and characteristics (such as people's ages or backgrounds) effectively enough to stratify the sample properly.

> No method can guarantee a representative sample, but you should have confidence that your sample is (quite) representative if you want to generalise your results to the entire target group.

Participants Sometimes *Act Differently* When They're Being *Observed*

Human participants will usually be aware that they are being **studied**. This may mean they don't show their **true response**, and so their data may not be **valid** or **reliable**. Some of these effects are explained below...

1 **THE HAWTHORNE EFFECT**: If people are **interested** in something and in the attention they are getting (e.g. from researchers), then they show a more **positive** response, try **harder** at tasks, and so on.

   This means their results for tests are often **artificially high** (because they're trying harder than normal), which could make a researcher's conclusions **invalid**.

   The opposite effect may occur if the participants are **uninterested** in the task.

2 **DEMAND CHARACTERISTICS**: There are aspects of a study which allow the participants to form an idea about its **purpose**. If they think they know what kind of response the researcher is **expecting** from them, they may show that response to '**please**' the researcher (or they may **deliberately** do the **opposite**). Either way, the conclusions drawn from the study would be **invalid**.

3 **SOCIAL DESIRABILITY BIAS**: People usually try to show themselves in the **best possible light**. So in a survey, they may **not** be completely **truthful**, but give answers that are more **socially acceptable** instead (e.g. people may say they give more money to charity than they really do). This would make the results **less valid**.

Selecting and Using Participants

The Researchers Can Affect the Outcomes in Undesirable Ways

The **reliability** and **validity** of results may also be influenced by the researcher, since he or she has **expectations** about what will happen. This can produce the following effects:

1   RESEARCHER (or EXPERIMENTER) BIAS: The researchers' **expectations** can influence how they **design** their study and how they **behave** towards the participants. Also, their expectations may influence **how** they take **measurements** and **analyse** their data, resulting in errors that can lead, for example, to accepting a hypothesis that was actually false. Their expectations may also lead them to only ask questions about what **they** are **interested** in, and they may **focus** on the aspects of the participant's answers which **fit** their **expectations**.

2   INVESTIGATOR EFFECTS: These can be anything that the researcher does which can affect how the participant **behaves**. If a researcher's expectations influence how they behave towards their participants, the participants might respond to **demand characteristics**. Also, a researcher's **expectations** could result in them asking **leading questions**. Finally, the participant may react to the **behaviour** or **appearance** of an investigator and answer differently.

Practice Questions

Q1   What is random sampling?
Q2   Give a disadvantage of opportunity sampling.
Q3   Give an advantage of volunteer sampling.
Q4   What is a systematic sample?
Q5   Give a disadvantage of stratified sampling.
Q6   What are demand characteristics?
Q7   Give an example of experimenter bias.

Exam Questions

Q1   Describe one advantage of using a systematic sample.   [2 marks]

Q2   Read the item below and then answer the questions that follow.

> A psychologist was investigating the relationship between the number of sick-days taken by Year 12 students over one academic year and their final exam results.
>
> A sample of 50 Year 12 students was taken from one school. Their absences over the whole year, as recorded in the daily register, were correlated with the results of their final exam taken at the end of Year 12.

   a)   Describe how the psychologist could have used random sampling to select the participants.   [2 marks]

   b)   Outline one disadvantage of using random sampling to select participants.   [2 marks]

   c)   Describe another sampling technique which could have made the sample more representative than random sampling.   [3 marks]

Q3   Outline the effects of demand characteristics on scientific research.   [2 marks]

Q4   Outline how investigator effects might influence the outcome of a psychological study.   [2 marks]

Volunteers needed for study into pain and embarrassment... (and stupidity)

Bear in mind that loads of the studies here were done in universities. Students are pretty easy to get your hands on in universities, so they make up most of the samples. Trouble is, students are quite different to the rest of the population (lots of beans on toast, sleeping through the day, you know the type) so the samples could be pretty unrepresentative...

Ethical Issues in Psychological Research

Remember Milgram's obedience research? The one that made participants think they were giving lethal electric shocks to others. It was a bit... "unethical", some might say. If you're not sure what that means, worry not, just read on...

Ethics are an Important Issue in Psychology

Psychological research and practice should aim to improve our **self-understanding**, be **beneficial** to people and try to **improve the quality of life** for individuals. As professionals, psychologists are expected to do their work in an **ethical manner**.

The British Psychological Society (BPS) Produces Ethical Guidelines

The **British Psychological Society** (BPS) has developed ethical guidelines for psychologists to follow when they're designing studies, so that participants are protected. They are **formal principles** for what is considered to be acceptable or unacceptable, and include advice on **deception**, **consent** and **psychological harm**.

1 Informed Consent	• BPS guidelines state that participants should always give **informed consent**. • They should be told the aims and nature of the study before agreeing to it. • They should also know that they have the **right to withdraw** at any time.

1) **BUT** if the participant is under 16 years of age they can't **legally** give consent (although a parent can).

2) In **naturalistic observation** studies, consent is not obtained. In this case the research is acceptable provided that it is done in a **public location** where people would expect to be observed by others.

3) Even when informed consent is supposedly obtained, issues may be raised. **Menges (1973)** reviewed about 1000 American studies and found that **97%** had not given people all the information about the research.

2 Deception	• If participants have been deceived then they cannot have given **informed consent**. • However, sometimes researchers must **withhold information** about the study because the participants wouldn't behave **naturally** if they knew what the aim was.

1) The BPS guidelines state that deception is only acceptable if there is strong **scientific justification** for the research and there's **no alternative procedure** available to obtain the data.

2) Researchers can also ask **independent people** if they would object to the study. If they wouldn't, it may be done with naïve participants (although they **may not agree** with others' opinions about the study).

3) Participants could just be given **general** details — although if too little is said they may feel **deceived** (but if participants know too much then they may not behave naturally).

4) The **severity** of deception differs, e.g. research on memory may involve **unexpected** memory tests (that participants weren't informed about). This is **less objectionable** than the deception involved in Milgram's study.

3 Protection from harm	• The BPS guidelines say that the risk of harm to participants should be **no greater** than they would face in their normal lives. It's hard to **accurately assess** this.

1) Research procedures can involve physical and psychological discomfort, e.g. **Glass and Singer (1972)** exposed participants to noise to make them stressed, and participants in **Milgram's** research suffered extreme distress.

2) Some people face **risks** in their work (e.g. soldiers), but that doesn't mean they can be exposed to risks in research.

3) Researchers don't always **know in advance** what might be distressing for participants.

Ethical Issues in Psychological Research

<table>
<tr><td>4   Debriefing</td><td>•   Debriefing is supposed to return participants to the state they were in **before the research**.
•   It's especially important if **deception** has been used.</td></tr>
</table>

1)   Researchers must fully explain what the research involved and what the results might show.
2)   Participants are given the **right to withdraw their data**.

<table>
<tr><td>5   Confidentiality</td><td>•   None of the participants in a psychological study should be **identifiable** from any reports that are produced.</td></tr>
</table>

1)   Data collected during research must be **confidential** — researchers can't use people's **names** in reports.
2)   Participants must be **warned** if their data is not going to be completely anonymous.
3)   However, some groups or people might be **easily identifiable** from their **characteristics** — more so if the report says where and when the study was carried out, etc.

Researchers *Have to Deal with* Ethical Issues in Their Studies

Deception

Sometimes it's difficult to conduct meaningful research without a bit of **deception**. If participants know exactly what's being studied then their behaviour might change, and the data you get would be useless.

Psychologists don't usually tell participants every last detail, but they do try to minimise deception. That way participants aren't likely to be upset when they find out the true nature of the study.

Milgram's experiment (page 7) is an example of a study that would probably not be considered ethical today. He deceived participants about the true purpose of the study and many of them showed signs of **stress** when taking part.

Consent

Gaining consent is central to conducting research ethically. But telling participants they're being observed could **change** the way they **behave**.

Milgram's participants couldn't give informed consent until after they were debriefed. If they'd known about the nature of the study, it wouldn't have worked.

Animal Rights *are Also an* Ethical Issue

Research with non-human animals has caused heated debate.

1)   In **support**, people argue that animal research has provided **valuable information** for psychological and medical research. Some **experimental designs** couldn't have been conducted on humans — e.g. Harlow's study on attachment, where young monkeys were separated from their mothers and reared alone (page 28).

2)   Some **disagree** with the idea of conducting research with non-human animals. They may argue that it's **ethically wrong** to inflict harm and suffering on animals, and obviously animals can't give consent to take part.

3)   Some argue that it's cruel to experiment on animals that have a **similar intelligence** to humans, because they might suffer the same problems we would. It'd be OK to experiment on animals that are far less developed than us, but there is no point because they'll be **too different** from us to give results that apply to humans.

Ethical Issues in Psychological Research

Ethical Guidelines **Don't Solve** All the Problems

1) There may be researchers who **don't follow the guidelines** properly. Naughty.

2) If a psychologist conducts research in an unacceptable way, they **can't be banned** from research (unlike a doctor who can be 'struck off' for misconduct). But they'd probably be kicked out of their university and the BPS.

3) Even when guidelines are followed, it can be **difficult to assess** things like **psychological harm**, or to **fully justify the use of deception**.

4) Deciding whether the ends (benefits from the study) justify the means (how it was done and at what cost) is not straightforward either. This creates another dilemma for psychologists.

The lasting harm to Milgram's participants was beginning to show.

Practice Questions

Q1 What are 'ethical guidelines' and why are they needed in psychology?
Q2 Why is it sometimes impossible to obtain informed consent from participants?
Q3 If you have used deception, what should you do immediately after the study?
Q4 For the issue of psychological harm, what level of risk is said to be acceptable in research?
Q5 What is the purpose of debriefing?
Q6 Why might people disagree with the idea of conducting non-human animal research?

Exam Questions

Q1 Read the item below, then answer the question that follows.

> A psychologist aims to investigate the relationship between anxiety and response time. The psychologist will ask participants to either watch a calm or frightening movie clip, then respond to a series of cognitive tasks.

Outline why the participants would need debriefing after this study. [2 marks]

Q2 Read the item below, then answer the question that follows.

> A researcher wants to study the effect of sleep deprivation on memory. He intends to divide participants into two groups and ask them to learn a list of 15 words. The first group will then be deprived of sleep for 24 hours, whilst the second group will maintain a normal level of rest.
>
> Both groups will then be asked to recall the list of words.

Outline at least **two** ethical principles that will need to be considered for this psychological research, as developed by the British Psychological Society. [6 marks]

Don't let someone debrief you unless you love them very much...

Psychological experiments create many ethical dilemmas. Take Milgram's study — there's no doubting that the results reveal interesting things about how people interact. But do these results justify the possible psychological damage done to the participants? There's no right or wrong answer, but the BPS guidelines are there to address this issue exactly.

The Scientific Process

The scientific process is all about how we develop and test scientific ideas. It's what scientists do all day, every day. Well, except at coffee time. Never come between scientists and their coffee.

Science Answers Real-life Questions

Science tries to explain **how** and **why** things happen — it **answers questions**. It's all about seeking and gaining **knowledge** about the world around us. Scientists do this by **asking** questions and **suggesting** answers and then **testing** them to see if they're correct — this is the **scientific process**.

The evidence supported Reggie's Theory of Flammable Burps.

1) **Ask** a question — make an **observation** and ask **why or how** it happens.

2) **Suggest** an answer, or part of an answer, by forming a **theory** (a possible explanation of the observations).

3) Make a **prediction** or **hypothesis** — a **specific testable statement**, based on the theory, about what will happen in a test situation.

4) Carry out a **test** — to provide **evidence** that will support the prediction (or help to disprove it).

Suggesting explanations is all very well and good, but if there's **no way to test** them then it just ain't science. A theory is **only scientific** if it can be tested.

Science is All About Testing Theories

It starts off with one experiment backing up a prediction and theory. It ends up with all the scientists in the world **agreeing** with it and you **learning** it. Stirring stuff. This is how the magical process takes place:

1) The results are **published** — scientists need to let others know about their work, so they try to get their results published in **scientific journals**. These are just like normal magazines, only they contain **scientific reports** (called papers) instead of celebrity gossip. All work must undergo **peer review** before it's published.

- **Peer review** is a process used to help **ensure the integrity** of published scientific work. Before publication, scientific work is sent to **experts** in that field (**peers**) so they can assess the **quality** of the work.

- This process helps to keep scientists **honest** — e.g. you can't 'sex-up' your conclusions if the data doesn't support it, because it **won't pass** peer review.

- Peer review helps to **validate conclusions** — it means published theories, data and conclusions are more trustworthy. But it **can't guarantee** that the conclusions are 100% right. More **rounds** of predicting and testing are needed before they can be taken as '**fact**'.

- Sometimes **mistakes** are made and bad science is published. Peer review **isn't perfect** but it's probably the best way for scientists to **self-regulate** their work and to ensure **reliable** scientific work is **published**.

2) Other scientists read the published theories and results, and try to **repeat them** — this involves repeating the **exact experiments**, and using the theory to make **new predictions** that are tested by **new experiments**.

3) If all the experiments in all the world provide evidence to back it up, the theory is thought of as scientific 'fact' (**for now**).

4) If **new evidence** comes to light that **conflicts** with the current evidence the theory is questioned all over again. More rounds of **testing** will be carried out to see which evidence, and so which theory, **prevails**.

The Scientific Process

Theories Get **Tested** Over and Over and Over and *Over and...*

Our currently accepted theories have survived this '**trial by evidence**'. They've been tested **over and over and over** and each time the results have backed them up. **BUT**, and this is a big but (teehee), they never become totally indisputable fact. Scientific **breakthroughs or advances** could provide new ways to question and test a theory, which could lead to **changes and challenges** to it. Then the testing starts all over again...

And this, my friend, is the **tentative nature of scientific knowledge** — it's always **changing** and **evolving**.

Psychological Research Can Impact the *Economy*

Psychologists conduct research into a wide range of areas. Their findings could have implications for the **economy**.

E.g. People with untreated mental health disorders may need more time off work

- People suffering from conditions like **depression** or **obsessive-compulsive disorder** which aren't being treated may need to take more days off work than those who are receiving treatment. **Treatments** for mental health disorders come about as a result of **psychological research** (e.g. cognitive-behaviour therapy, antidepressants, etc.), and can **help** people continue a normal lifestyle, such as going to **work**. Less time off work is **better** for the economy.

E.g. Research into sleep behaviour can help shift workers

- Modern work patterns mean some people work shifts throughout the 24-hour period, disrupting their **sleep cycle**.
- **Czeisler et al (1982)** studied workers at a factory whose shift patterns appeared to cause sleep and health problems. The researchers recommended **rotating shifts** every **21 days** (allowing more time for workers to adapt), and changing shifts forward in time (phase delay). The employees had previously worked a backwards rotation — working during the nights for the first week, late afternoons in the second week and only mornings during the third week (phase advance). They would then restart the pattern again in the fourth week.
- After implementing the changes, **productivity** and **job satisfaction** increased.
- **More productive** workers lead to a **better** economy.

Practice Questions

Q1 Briefly outline the scientific process.
Q2 Where are reports of psychological research usually published?
Q3 What happens when new evidence disproves a current psychological theory?
Q4 What happens when new evidence supports a current psychological theory?
Q5 Who conducted research into shift patterns?

Exam Questions

Q1 Outline why research should undergo a peer review before it is published. [2 marks]

Q2 Briefly discuss the implications of psychological research for the economy. [6 marks]

Happy people make a happy place to work...

Or is it the other way around? A happy place to work makes happy people? Either way, a happy and productive workforce is much more likely to influence the economy in a positive way. So if psychological research can figure out how to make people super-happy all of the time, we'll be rolling in it before you can say 'spaghetti bolognese'...

Descriptive Statistics

Run for your lives... panic. This really looks like maths... Well, actually, it's not too bad. So calm down.

Descriptive Statistics — Just Say What You See...

1) **Descriptive statistics** simply describe the **patterns** found in a set of data.

2) Descriptive statistics uses the fancy term '**central tendency**' to describe an **average**.   For example, the central tendency (average) for the height of a group of 18-year-old boys might be about 1.70 metres.

3) Measures of **dispersion** describe **how spread out** the data is.
   For example, the difference in height between the shortest 18-year-old boy and the tallest might be 35 cm.

There are 3 Measures of Central Tendency (aka Average) You Need to Know

The Mean — This is the 'Normal Average'

You calculate the **mean** by **adding** all of the scores in a data set and then **dividing** by the number of scores.

$$\text{Mean} = \bar{X} = \frac{\sum X}{N}, \text{ where } \sum X \text{ is the sum of all the scores (and there are } N \text{ of them).}$$

EXAMPLE:

If you've got scores of 2, 5, 6, 7 and 10, then...

$\sum X = 30$ (since all the scores add up to 30),

and $N = 5$ (since there are 5 of them)...

...so the **mean** is $\bar{X} = \dfrac{30}{5} = 6$

Remember to change N to the number of values in the data set.

EXAMPLE:

If you've got scores of 34, 45, 2, 37, 11, 53 and 19, then...

$\sum X = 201$ (since all the scores add up to 201),

and $N = 7$ (since there are 7 of them)...

...so the **mean** is $\bar{X} = \dfrac{201}{7} = \mathbf{28.71}$

Σ (pronounced 'sigma') just means you add things up.

ADVANTAGES:

a) It uses **all** the scores in a data set.

b) It's used in **further calculations** and so it's handy to work it out.

DISADVANTAGES:

a) It can be **skewed** (distorted) by extremely **high** or **low** scores. This can make it **unrepresentative** of most of the scores, and so it may be **misleading**. In these cases, it's best not to use the mean. For example, the scores 10, 40, 25, 20 and 650 have a mean of 149, which is not representative of the central tendency of the data set.

b) It can sometimes give an **unrealistically precise** value (e.g. the average family has 2.4 children — but what does 0.4 of a child mean...?).

The Mode — The Score that Occurs Most Often

EXAMPLE:

The mode (or the modal score) of 2, 5, 2, 9, 6, 11 and 2 is **2**.

If there are two scores which are most common then the data set is 'bimodal'. If there are three or more scores which are most common then the data set is 'multimodal'.

ADVANTAGES:

a) It shows the **most common** or 'important' score.

b) It's always a result from the actual **data set**, so it can be a more **useful** or **realistic** statistic, e.g. the modal average family has 2 children, not 2.4.

DISADVANTAGES:

a) It's not very useful if there are **several** modal values, or if the modal value is only **slightly** more common than other scores.

b) It has **little further use** in data analysis.

Descriptive Statistics

The Median — *The **Middle Score** When the Data is Put in **Order***

EXAMPLE:

The **median** of the scores 4, 5, 10, 12 and 14 is **10**.

In the above example there was **one score** in the **middle**, as there was an odd number of scores.
If there is an even number of scores, there will be **two** middle scores.
Add them together and then **divide by 2** to get the median:

EXAMPLE:

The **median** of the scores 2, 6, 27, 45, 52 and 63 is **36**.
In this example there are two middle scores (27 and 45).
So you do: 27 + 45 = 72, 72 ÷ 2 = **36**

> Don't forget to arrange the
> scores in numerical order first.

ADVANTAGES:

a)   It's relatively **quick** and **easy** to calculate.

b)   It's **not** affected by extremely high or low
     scores, so it can be used on 'skewed' sets of
     data to give a 'representative' average score.

DISADVANTAGES:

a)   Not **all** the scores are used to work out the median.

b)   It has **little further use** in data analysis.

*Measures of **Dispersion** Tell You How **Spread Out** the Data Is*

Range — *Highest Score Minus the Lowest Score*

EXAMPLE:

The **range** of the scores 6, 10, 35 and 50 is 50 – 6 = **44**.

ADVANTAGE:

It's **quick** and **easy** to calculate.

DISADVANTAGE:

It completely ignores the **central** values of a data set, so
it can be misleading if there are very **high** or **low** scores.

1)   The **interquartile range (IQR)** can be calculated to help **avoid** this disadvantage.

2)   First the **median** is identified (this is sometimes called **Q2**).

3)   If there's an **odd** number of values then you take the middle number as the median.
     If there's an **even** number of values then you take the 2 middle numbers, add them together
     and divide them by 2 to find the median.

4)   The **median** of the **lower half** of the data is called the **lower quartile** (or **Q1**).
     The **median** of the **upper half** of the data is called the **upper quartile** (or **Q3**).

5)   The **IQR = Q3 – Q1**.

EXAMPLE:

Look at the data set: 3, 3, **4**, 5, 6, **8**, 10, 13, **14**, 16, 19.

There are 11 values, so median (Q2) = 6th value = **8**.

Then Q1 = **4**, Q3 = **14**, and so IQR = 14 – 4 = **10**.

Tom had conquered the range.
In more ways than one.

Descriptive Statistics

Standard Deviation — Measures, on Average, How Much Scores Deviate from the Mean

$$s = \sqrt{\frac{\sum (X - \bar{X})^2}{N}}, \text{ where } s = \text{standard deviation}$$

Remember — $\bar{X}$ is the mean.

EXAMPLE:

If you've got scores of 5, 9, 10, 11 and 15, then...

Start by working out the mean: $(5 + 9 + 10 + 11 + 15) \div 5 = 50 \div 5 = 10$.

Now put the numbers into the formula to find the standard deviation:

$$s = \sqrt{\frac{(5-10)^2 + (9-10)^2 + (10-10)^2 + (11-10)^2 + (15-10)^2}{5}} = \textbf{3.22} \text{ (3 s.f.)}$$

A high standard deviation shows more variability in a set of data.

This answer just means that the scores in the data set are, on average, 3.22 away from the mean.

ADVANTAGES:

a) **All** scores in the set are taken into account, so it's **more accurate** than the range.

b) It can also be used in further analysis.

DISADVANTAGE:

It's **not** as quick or easy to calculate as the range.

Practice Questions

Q1 Explain how to calculate the mean.

Q2 What is the difference between the mean and the mode?

Q3 How is the range calculated?

Q4 What is meant by 'standard deviation'?

Exam Questions

Q1 Work out the mean, median and mode for the following data set: 2, 2, 4, 6, 8, 9, 10. [3 marks]

Q2 Which of the following is a measure of dispersion?
A standard deviation   **B** mean   **C** median   **D** mode   [1 mark]

Q3 Read the item below and then answer the questions that follow.

Sarah was investigating the effect of caffeine on typing speed. Her results are shown in Table 1.

Table 1: Time taken by 10 participants to type five sentences.

	Time to type five sentences (seconds)									
Before Caffeine	20	18	15	12	11	9	15	15	14	12
After Caffeine	30	24	12	10	15	12	28	30	20	12

a) Calculate the range of the scores after the participants had taken caffeine. [1 mark]

b) Calculate the mean for the participants' scores before caffeine. [2 marks]

Did you know, 99.99% of statistics are made up...

These statistics are used to describe a collection of scores in a data set (how big the scores are, how spread out they are, and so on), so they're called... wait for it... descriptive statistics. Don't be put off by the weirdy maths notation either — a bar on top of a letter (e.g. $\bar{X}$) means you work out the mean. And a sigma (Σ) means you add things up.

Correlations and Distributions

You know what they say — correlation is as correlation does.
Remember that as you read this page... then you won't go far wrong.

Correlation Measures How Closely Two Variables are Related

1) **Correlation** is a measure of the relationship between **two variables**, e.g. it can tell you how closely exam grades are related to the amount of revision that someone's done.

2) In a **correlational study** data is collected for some kind of **correlational analysis**.

The Correlation Coefficient is a Number Between −1 and +1

1) To find the correlation between two variables, you first have to collect some **data**.

   For example, you could ask every student in a class how many hours of study they did each week, and note their average test result.

Student	Hours of study	Average test score — %
A	4	58
B	1	23
C	7	67
D	15	89

2) You can then work out a **correlation coefficient**. This is a number between −1 and +1, and shows:

   a) **How closely** the variables are linked. This is shown by the **size** of the number — if it's **close** to +1 or −1, then they are **very closely** related, while a smaller number means the relationship is **less strong** (or maybe not there at all if it's close to 0).

   b) The **type** of correlation — a **positive** correlation coefficient (i.e. between 0 and +1) means that the variables rise and fall together, while a negative correlation coefficient (i.e. between −1 and 0) means that as one variable rises, the other falls. (See below for more info.)

Correlation is Easy to See on Scattergrams

1) **Positive correlation** — this means that as one variable rises, so does the other (and likewise, if one falls, so does the other).
   Example: hours of study and average test score.
   The correlation coefficient is roughly **0.75** (close to +1).

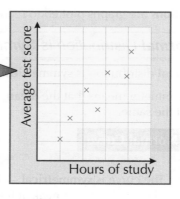

2) **Negative correlation** — this means that as one variable rises, the other one falls (and vice versa).
   Example: hours of TV watched each week and average test score.
   The correlation coefficient is roughly **−0.75** (close to −1).

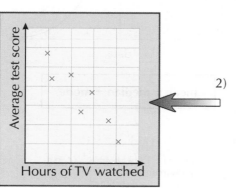

3) **Zero correlation** — if the correlation coefficient is 0 (or close to 0), then the two variables aren't linked.
   Example: students' heights and their average test scores.
   The correlation coefficient is roughly **0.01** (close to 0).

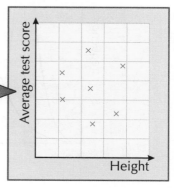

Correlations and Distributions

Correlational Research has some Advantages...

1) Because correlational research doesn't involve **controlling** any variables, you can do it when (for **practical** or **ethical** reasons) you couldn't do a **controlled experiment**. Handy.

2) For example, an experiment into the effects of smoking on humans probably wouldn't be done for ethical reasons, but a correlation between smoking and cancer could be established from hospital records.

3) Correlational analysis can give ideas for **future** research (e.g. biological research on the effects of smoking).

4) Correlation can even be used to test for **reliability** and **validity** (e.g. by testing the results of the same test taken twice by the same people — a good **reliable** test will show a **high correlation**).

...but some Limitations

1) Correlational analysis **can't** establish '**cause and effect**' relationships — it can only show that there's a **statistical link** between variables. Variables can be closely correlated without changes in one causing changes in the other — a **third variable** could be involved. Only a **controlled experiment** can show cause-and-effect relationships.

2) Care must be taken when **interpreting** correlation coefficients — high correlation coefficients could be down to **chance**. To decide whether a coefficient is **significant**, you have to use a proper **significance test** (see p.104-105).

For example, the number of births in a town was found to be positively correlated to the number of storks that nested in that town — but that didn't mean that more storks caused the increase.

(It was because more people in the town led to more births, and also to more houses with chimneys to nest on.)

Normal and Skewed Distributions Look Very Different

Distributions are graphs plotted to represent the **average** and **spread** of some **characteristic** of the population.

A Normal Distribution is Symmetrical

A **normal** distribution is **symmetrical** about the **mean**.

This symmetry means that the **mean**, **median** and **mode** are all the **same**.

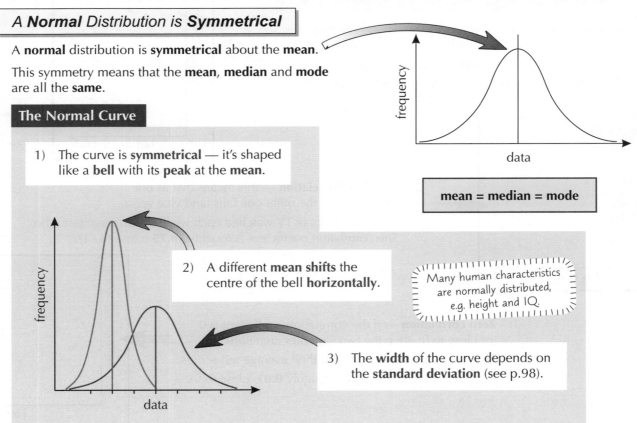

mean = median = mode

The Normal Curve

1) The curve is **symmetrical** — it's shaped like a **bell** with its **peak** at the **mean**.

2) A different **mean** shifts the centre of the bell **horizontally**.

Many human characteristics are normally distributed, e.g. height and IQ.

3) The **width** of the curve depends on the **standard deviation** (see p.98).

Correlations and Distributions

A *Skewed* Distribution can be *Positive* or *Negative*

When there are **scores** that **cluster** together at either end of the data, it results in a **skewed distribution**.

Positive Skew

If data is **positively skewed**, there is a cluster of scores at the **lower** end of the data set.

The curve has a tail on the **right** side of the peak — it is said to be **skewed to the right**.

The mode is **less than** the median, which is **less than** the mean.

Examples are **reaction times**, the number of **children** in a family, and **income**.

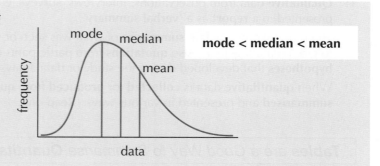

mode < median < mean

Negative Skew

For a **negative** skew, there are **more** scores at the **higher** end of the data set.

The tail is on the **left** side of the peak — it is skewed **to the left**.

The mode is **more than** the median, which is **more than** the mean.

Negative skew is less common but an example is **age at retirement**.

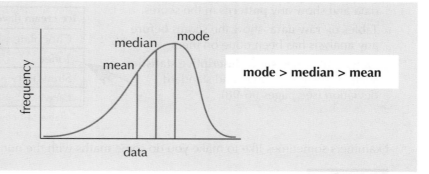

mode > median > mean

Practice Questions

Q1 Explain what is meant by correlation.

Q2 What is a correlation coefficient?

Q3 What two things are shown by a correlation coefficient?

Q4 Explain the difference between a negative correlation and no correlation.

Q5 What does a normal distribution curve look like?

Q6 Is the mean greater or less than the mode in a positively skewed distribution?

Exam Questions

Q1 A study has found a negative correlation between tiredness and reaction time.
Explain what this means.

[1 mark]

Q2 Outline why psychologists cannot use correlational research to draw conclusions such as
"eating an apple every day increases life expectancy".

[2 marks]

Q3 Read the item below and then answer the question that follows.

> 50 participants were asked to complete a personality questionnaire to see how introverted they were.
> The mean score for the group was 4.5, the modal score was 8 and the median score was 6.

What type of distribution would these results show?

[1 mark]

Stats sucks...

Look at the graphs showing the large positive and large negative correlations — all the points lie close-ish to a straight line, which slopes either upwards (positive correlation) or downwards (negative correlation). And don't forget about distributions too. Normal curves are symmetrical and skewed curves have tails. Not real tails obviously. That'd be odd.

Summarising Data

It's not very scientific or anything, but the only bit about statistics I don't find mind-numbingly boring is the bit where you get to make all the lovely numbers look pretty... Ignore me — stats has turned my brain to mush.

Data Can be Presented in Various Ways

1) **Qualitative** data from observations, interviews, surveys, etc. (see pages 83-85) can be presented in a **report** as a 'verbal summary'.

2) The report would contain **summaries** of what was seen or said, possibly using **categories** to group data together. Also **quotations** from participants can be used, and any **research hypotheses** that developed during the study or data analysis may be discussed.

3) When **quantitative** data is **collected** (or **produced** from **qualitative** data) it can be **summarised** and presented in various ways. Read on...

Tables are a Good Way to Summarise Quantitative Data

Tables can be used to clearly present the data and show any **patterns** in the scores.

Tables of '**raw data**' show the scores **before** any **analysis** has been done on them.

Other tables may show **descriptive statistics** such as the mean, range and standard deviation (see pages 96-98).

Ice cream flavour	Quality (score out of 10)		
	Tastiness	Thickness	Throwability
Chocolate	5	7	6
Toffee	8	6	7
Strawberry	6	5	4
Earwax	6	9	8

Table to Show the Qualities of Different Flavour Ice Cream

Examiners sometimes like to make you do some **maths** with the numbers in **tables** and **graphs**.

EXAMPLE:

What **percentage** of the participants who obeyed were boys?

	Boys	Girls
Number of participants who obeyed	36	24
Number of participants who didn't obey	52	64

To find the percentage, divide the number of boys who obeyed by the total number of participants who obeyed, then multiply by 100.

Find the total number of participants who obeyed: 36 + 24 = 60

Percentage of boys among those who obeyed: (36 ÷ 60) × 100 = **60%**

Mr Boggis's data was summarised nicely on his table.

Line Graphs are Good for Showing More Than One Set of Data

Line graphs are for use with **continuous data**. The **independent variable** is plotted along the **x-axis** and the **dependent variable** is plotted up the **y-axis**.

They show the plotted data points, which are then **joined up** with **straight lines**.

It can be useful to combine **two or more** line graphs on the same set of axes — then it's easy to **make comparisons** between groups.

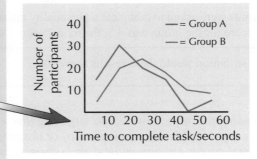

If you need to plot a line graph, you'll get marks for labelling the axes (including the units), accurate plotting, and including a title.

Summarising Data

Nearly done — just a little bit more...

Bar Charts Can be Used for Non-continuous Data

Bar chart showing the mean number of words recalled by two groups in a memory experiment.

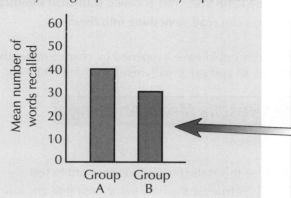

Bar charts are usually used to present '**non-continuous data**' (like when a variable falls into **categories** rather than being measured on a numbered scale).

This bar chart shows the mean number of words recalled by different groups in a memory experiment. Note that the columns in bar charts **don't touch** each other. Also, it's preferable to always show the **full vertical scale**, or **clearly indicate** when it isn't all shown (otherwise it can be **misleading**).

Scattergrams Can Tell You if Two Variables are Related

Scattergrams are used when you've got **two different variables** — you plot one variable along the bottom of the graph, and the second one up the side. Scattergrams are good for showing whether there's a **correlation** (see p.99).

EXAMPLE:

Gill is investigating the relationship between height and scores on a depression index.

Height (cm)	Depression Score
150	20
164	32
100	10
130	18
140	30

- Choose a suitable scale for each axis.

- Carefully plot the data points — but don't join them up.

- Instead, you can draw a line of best fit to show a trend — draw a line which passes through or as near to as many of the points as possible.

Practice Questions

Q1 What kind of information is typically shown in tables?

Q2 What kind of data is shown on bar charts?

Exam Questions

Q1 A sample of children were observed in an observational study. Their attachment styles were recorded below.

	Secure	Insecure-avoidant	Insecure-resistant
Number of children	56	17	7

Calculate the percentage of the children from the sample who had a secure attachment. [2 marks]

Q2 Draw a bar chart showing the percentage obedience for boys and girls from the table on page 102. [6 marks]

Is it too late to make a gag about Correlation Street...

Hmm, I think I've missed the boat with that one. But if you like it, maybe turn back a page and imagine I put it there instead. How we laughed. Now wipe away the tears of joy and let's think about the fun of summarising data. Here's one — what did the table say to the bar chart... Oh who am I kidding — let's just be thankful it's almost over...

Inferential Statistics

Inferential statistics let you make an 'inference' (or educated guess) about whether your results show something significant, or if they're due to chance. "Marvellous," I hear you cry. "Just what I've always wanted to learn about..."

Inferential Statistics are about Ruling Out Chance

1) You can never be 100% certain that results aren't all down to chance. So instead of 'proving' a hypothesis, you have to be content with finding out whether it's **likely** to be true. This is called **statistical significance**.

2) If your results are statistically significant, it means that you can **read something into them** — they're unlikely to be just down to chance.

3) If your results are **not statistically significant**, it means they could have happened by chance rather than being the effect of changes in your independent variable, so you can't really read anything into them.

Use *Statistical Tests* to Find Out if Your Results *Mean* Anything

OK, it's not easy, this bit — so stop texting people and concentrate...

1
- The first thing you do is write out your **null hypothesis** — this is the prediction you want to **test**.
- In a statistical test, you assume that your null hypothesis is **true** for the time being, and that any hint of a significant difference between your groups (or correlation between your variables) is actually just a **fluke**.

2
- Next you choose a **significance level** — this is a **'level of proof'** that you're looking for before you read anything into your results.
- The smaller the significance level, the stronger the evidence you're looking for that your results aren't just down to chance.
- A significance level is a **probability**, and so is a number between 0 and 1.
- (Probabilities near 1 mean things are very **likely**, and probabilities near 0 mean things are very **unlikely**.)
- Significance levels are always **very small** — usually 0.05 (5%) or less. (Because a significance level is very **small**, events with probabilities smaller than the significance level are very **unlikely** to happen.)

I didn't inhale, honest.

3
- You then turn all your experimental results into a single **test statistic** (see the next page).
- Then you can find out what the **probability** is that this test statistic, and therefore your results, were the result of a **fluke** (making your **null hypothesis true** after all).

4
- If the probability of your results being a fluke is **less than** the significance level (e.g. 5%), then it's pretty safe to say that your null hypothesis **wasn't actually true**. You can therefore assume that the **difference** you've noticed between your groups was down to the change you made in your **independent variable**.
- This is what stats-folk mean when they talk about 'rejecting the null hypothesis'. (If you reject your null hypothesis, you assume your **alternative hypothesis** is true instead.)

5
- If you reject your null hypothesis, you can proudly shout out that your results are **statistically significant**.

6
- If you **don't reject** the null hypothesis, it means that your results could have occurred **by chance**, rather than because your null hypothesis was wrong.
- If this happens, you've proved **nothing** — not rejecting the null hypothesis doesn't mean it **must be true**.

7
- Using a significance level of **0.05** (5%) is okay for most tests.
- If the probability of your results being down to chance is **less than** or **equal to** this ($p \leq 0.05$), then it's **pretty good evidence** that the null hypothesis **wasn't true** after all. So the researchers can be at least **95% confident** in their conclusion.
- If you use a significance level of **0.01** (1%), then you're looking for **really strong evidence** that the null hypothesis is untrue before you're going to reject it. The researchers can be at least **99% confident**.

Inferential Statistics

There are *Various Ways* to *Test Significance*

1) **Inferential statistical tests** help you decide whether to accept or reject the null hypothesis.
2) You calculate a **test statistic** which you can then compare against a **critical value**, which is provided for each test in a **critical value table**. This indicates whether or not the results are **significant**.

You Can Use the *Sign Test* to Look for *Significance*

One of the easiest statistical tests to use is the **sign test**.
It compares scores in data from **repeated measures** or **matched pairs** designs.

Example:	The impact of a drug treatment for depression is investigated in a **repeated measures** design.

Depression Index (1-20)	Participant no.	1	2	3	4	5	6	7	8
	Before Treatment	12	5	6	8	10	12	15	9
	After Treatment	5	6	4	2	3	2	16	9

1) The **difference** between each participant's two scores is calculated:

Participant no.	1	2	3	4	5	6	7	8
Difference	7	1	2	6	7	10	1	0
Sign (+/-)	–	+	–	–	–	–	+	

Always subtract in the same direction, noting if the result is a positive or negative value. Any differences of zero are removed from the results.

2) You then indicate whether the change was **positive** or **negative**.
3) Add up the number of positive signs and negative signs. The **smallest** one is the **test statistic**.

Negative signs are where the patient was less depressed after treatment and positive signs are where the patient was more depressed after treatment.

4) There are **5 negative** signs and **2 positive** signs. So the test statistic is **2**.
5) The test statistic must be **less than or equal to** the **critical value** to be significant.

- Critical values for each number of participants can be found in a **special table** that you'll be given.
- In this case, the **critical value** is 0. Since the test statistic is **greater than** 0, the results are **not significant**.
- The **null hypothesis** can't be **rejected**. There is **no significant difference** in the patients' depression scores before and after treatment. It's more than 5% likely that any improvement was down to **chance** rather than the drug.

Sandra wanted to work out the observed value but had totally forgotten which bottle was which.

Practice Questions

Q1 What does it mean if the results of an experiment or study are not statistically significant?
Q2 What two significance levels are often used in statistical tests?
Q3 Describe the steps of the sign test.

Exam Questions

Q1 Outline what is meant by $p \leq 0.05$. [2 marks]

Q2 Complete this sentence:
The observed test statistic in a sign test should be ...... the critical value to be considered significant.

A greater than or equal to   **B** less than   **C** greater than   **D** less than or equal to   [1 mark]

There's a high probability that you'll be able to infer this stuff is important...

So, got all that? If not, have a read back over the pages again until it sinks in. In a very small nutshell, you can't ever rule out the possibility that your results are down to chance, but you can conclude that the likelihood of that is as small as possible. And, joy of joys, there's a lovely statistical test to show you how it's done. I know, I know, I'm spoiling you.

Summary of the Exams

Here's what you can expect to see in your two AS Psychology exams.
AS exams are linear, so that means you'll do both exams at the end of the course.

The Exam Papers are **Broken Down** into Sections

Paper 1 — Introductory Topics in Psychology

Paper 1 is broken down into **three** sections, like this:

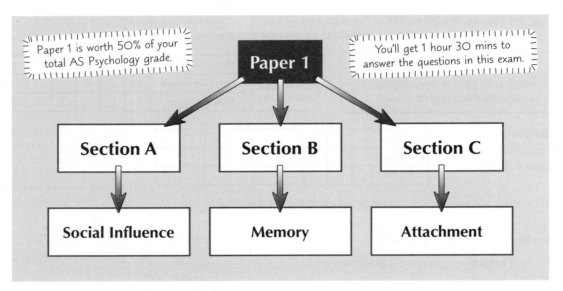

Paper 1 is worth 50% of your total AS Psychology grade.

You'll get 1 hour 30 mins to answer the questions in this exam.

Paper 1

Section A	Section B	Section C
Social Influence	Memory	Attachment

In each section you'll get **multiple choice questions**, **short answer questions** and at least one **extended writing question**.

Each section is worth **24 marks**, which means there are **72 marks** up for grabs in Paper 1.

Paper 2 — Psychology in Context

Paper 2 has **three** wonderful sections too:

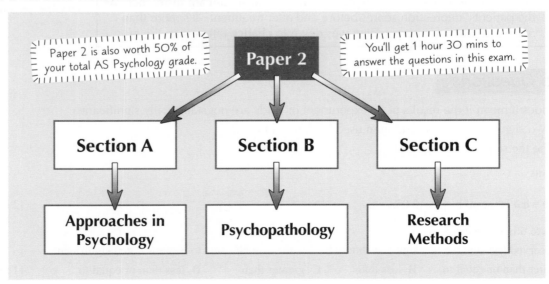

Paper 2 is also worth 50% of your total AS Psychology grade.

You'll get 1 hour 30 mins to answer the questions in this exam.

Paper 2

Section A	Section B	Section C
Approaches in Psychology	Psychopathology	Research Methods

This paper also has **multiple choice questions**, **short answer questions** and at least one **extended writing question** in each section.

Again, each section is worth **24 marks**, which means there are **72 marks** up for grabs in Paper 2.

Assessment Objectives

You can get loads of clues about your answers from the exam paper.

You Need to Meet Certain **Assessment Objectives**

There are three **assessment objectives** — **AO1**, **AO2** and **AO3**.

AO1 is about the facts and theories

Questions containing **AO1** marks cover your **knowledge and understanding of science**, its **processes**, **techniques** and **procedures**. You get marks by **recalling** and **describing** psychological knowledge, such as theories, studies and methods. What you don't need to do is evaluate the theory (unless the question tells you too) — that'd just be a **waste of time** that you could use elsewhere, and you **won't get any extra marks**.

AO2 gets you to apply your knowledge

Questions containing **AO2** marks are slightly different in that they get you to **apply your knowledge and understanding of science**, its **processes**, **techniques** and **procedures**. Rather than just recalling stuff, e.g. listing relevant experiments, you've got to **apply your knowledge** to the different situations or contexts.

You might have to apply your knowledge:

- to a **made-up example** given in the question — e.g. you might be given some information about a person suffering from depression and have to outline behavioural, cognitive or emotional characteristics from the description.
- to a **practical** situation — e.g. you might be given the results of a study about how different reinforcements lead to different behaviours and be asked to explain how these results show evidence for conditioning. So you'd need to apply your knowledge of conditioning to the information given.
- in a situation with **qualitative data** (see pages 85-86).
- in a situation with **quantitative data** (see pages 85-86).

AO3 is about analysing, interpreting and evaluating

In questions containing **AO3** marks you could be given scientific information, ideas or evidence and be asked to **analyse**, **interpret** and **evaluate** them. You might need to **evaluate** a study or theory, or **draw conclusions** from the results of an experiment. You could even be asked to give **suggestions** on how to make a study **better**. You'll also need to be able to **design** psychological **procedures**.

Watch out — a question could contain more than one assessment objective. You need to read the question carefully and work out what you're being asked to do. See the next page for more on this.

Each Paper Has a **Different Weighting** of Assessment Objectives

There aren't a set number of **AO1**, **AO2** and **AO3** marks in each paper.
But, in **Paper 1**, there are slightly **more AO1** marks than **AO2** or **AO3** marks.
In **Paper 2**, there are slightly **more AO2** marks than **AO1** or **AO3** marks.

		Assessment Objective		
		AO1	AO2	AO3
Weighting (%)	Paper 1	19–22	12–15	15–18
	Paper 2	14–17	18–21	13–16

At least **10%** of your grade will come from questions involving some **maths**. It won't be super hard maths, so don't panic, but it will cover maths you've learnt at GCSE. As long as you're comfortable with **basic arithmetic**, **handling data**, **algebra** and **graphs**, then you'll be fine. (And don't worry — you can take your calculator into the exams.)

25–30% of your grade will also come from questions on **research methods**. These questions won't just appear in **Paper 2** — they could crop up **anywhere** (see page 112), so make sure you know your stuff really well.

DO WELL IN YOUR EXAMS

Assessment Objectives

Exam questions contain **content words** and **command words**. The content words give away what the **topic** of the question is. A command word gives you an **instruction** of exactly what you need to do to answer the question. It's really **vital** that you know what they mean so that you can write the **correct** things in your answer. For example, if the question simply asks you to '**describe**' or '**outline**' something, you don't need to go into evaluating or explaining stuff.

Command words that you might find in the exam include:

Command word	What it means
Give/Write	Give a brief answer from memory or from the information in the question.
Name	Use a technical term to identify something.
Identify/State	Give a brief one or two word answer, or a short sentence.
Draw	Illustrate your answer with a diagram.
Label	Name parts of a diagram.
Calculate	Use maths to work out the value of something.
Analyse	Break down into characteristics and features.
Comment	Give a backed-up opinion.
Describe	Give details of something — it might be a theory, concept, process or study.
Outline	This requires less detail than 'describe' — it's more of a brief summary of something. Just give details of the main or important features. You don't need to go into too much depth.
Choose/Select/ Which is/What is	Pick from a range of answer options.
Explain	If a question asks you to explain, you need to give reasons for it and say why it is the case.
Discuss	This is a bit like a debate. Give evidence and examples for what you're saying, and support your points with explanations. These questions tend to be worth quite a lot of marks.
Evaluate	Weigh up the advantages and disadvantages, positives and negatives, or strengths and weaknesses. Keep your answer balanced — don't just concentrate on one side.
Compare	Outline the similarities and differences between two things.
Distinguish	Explain the differences between two or more things.
Complete	Finish the question by filling in the missing information.
Suggest	Present a solution or better way of doing something.
Design	Give details of how to carry out something, e.g. a study.
Justify	Give reasons for your answer, providing evidence to back up your ideas.
Consider	This is quite similar to 'evaluate' — your answer will involve weighing up the point that you've been asked to consider. Again, keep your comments balanced.

Command words can sometimes be **combined** together in a question.
For example, examiners will often ask you to 'outline **and** evaluate' or 'describe **and** explain' something.
Don't let this put you off — just break the question down into bits.
Start your answer with the **outline** or **describe** bit, and then **move on** to your **evaluation** or your **explanation**.

What You Need to Write

The **Number of Marks** Tells You **How Much to Write...**

1) The number of marks that a question is worth gives you a pretty good clue of **how much to write**.

2) You get **one mark per correct point** made, so if a question is worth four marks, make sure you write four decent points.

3) There's no point writing a massive answer for a question that's only worth a few marks — it's just a **waste of your time**.

4) For the longer extended writing questions, make sure that you've written **enough** to cover the right number of marks, but don't just waffle.

Martha suddenly realised that the question was worth 8 marks, not 88.

...But You Can't Just Write About **Anything**

1) It's important to remember that it's not just a case of blindly scribbling down **everything** you can think of that's related to the subject. Doing this just **wastes time**, and it doesn't exactly impress the examiner.

2) You only get marks for stuff that's **relevant** and **answers the question**.

3) So, make sure you read over the question a couple of times before you start writing so that you really understand what it's asking.

An **Example Answer** to Show You What to Aim for...

This is the sort of answer that would get you full marks.

> The model has three features, and the question's worth 6 marks. So, you'd just need to write enough about each feature to get you two marks. The answer might look short, but it's all you'd need to write.

1 Outline the features of the multi-store model of memory. [6 marks]

> The multi-store model proposes that memory is made up of three stores. These are the sensory register, the short-term store and the long-term store. The sensory register holds the information that is constantly being taken in from the environment, such as visual and auditory information. If you don't pay attention to this information, it will be lost from the sensory register. However, if you do pay attention to it, it will pass into short-term memory. Short-term memory has a limited and temporary capacity, but if the information in it is rehearsed, it will be transferred into long-term memory, which theoretically has an unlimited capacity and duration.

Make sure the information in your answer is relevant, and keep it concise.

Don't open with a general or meaningless sentence — get straight into gaining marks.

Stop writing once you've answered the question — don't add irrelevant detail to fill up the space.

...And an **Alternate Answer** to Show You What **Not** to Write...

I repeat... What **NOT** to write...

1 Outline the features of the multi-store model of memory. [6 marks]

> Atkinson and Shiffrin proposed the multi-store model. They thought that memory is made up of three stores — a sensory register, a short-term store and a long-term store. The sensory register holds information from the environment. If you don't listen to this information, it gets lost. If you do listen to it, it will pass into short-term memory. It's then turned into long-term memory. The primacy effect supports this model. You can remember the first few items on a list well. They have been better rehearsed and have moved to long-term memory. Also, if rehearsal is prevented, memory gets worse.

This first sentence is a bit irrelevant — it won't get you any marks.

You'd only need to give this detail if the question had asked you to evaluate the model — writing it is just a waste of time.

This could do with more detail to explain that STM only has a limited capacity, and rehearsal is needed to move information to LTM.

The second answer lacks the **detail** of the first — it only sketches over the features of the model. It wouldn't earn all the possible marks. Also, there's quite a bit of **irrelevant information** that wouldn't get you any marks.

Worked Exam

Over the next four pages we've given you some examples of the different styles of exam questions that you might come across. You'll get a mix of multiple choice questions, short answer questions and extended writing questions — so make sure you're familiar with them all.

Some Questions Will be Multiple Choice Questions

These questions give you some **answer options** and you just need to pick the right one.

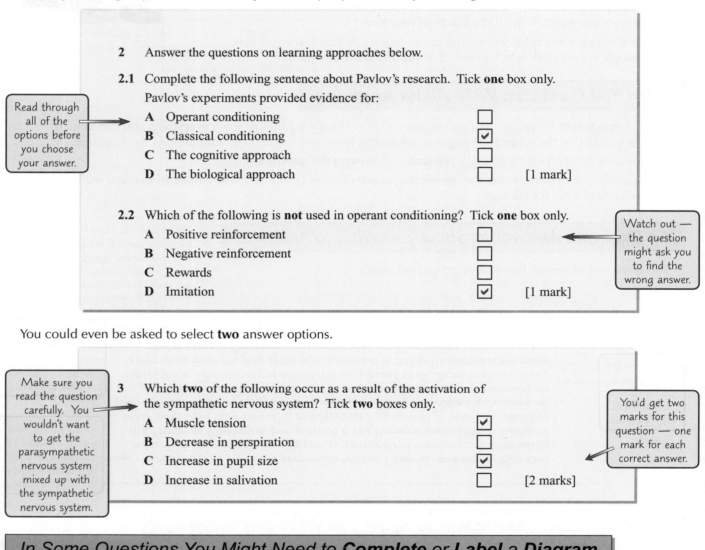

Read through all of the options before you choose your answer.

2   Answer the questions on learning approaches below.

2.1   Complete the following sentence about Pavlov's research. Tick **one** box only.
Pavlov's experiments provided evidence for:
A   Operant conditioning ☐
B   Classical conditioning ☑
C   The cognitive approach ☐
D   The biological approach ☐   [1 mark]

2.2   Which of the following is **not** used in operant conditioning? Tick **one** box only.
A   Positive reinforcement ☐
B   Negative reinforcement ☐
C   Rewards ☐
D   Imitation ☑   [1 mark]

Watch out — the question might ask you to find the wrong answer.

You could even be asked to select **two** answer options.

Make sure you read the question carefully. You wouldn't want to get the parasympathetic nervous system mixed up with the sympathetic nervous system.

3   Which **two** of the following occur as a result of the activation of the sympathetic nervous system? Tick **two** boxes only.
A   Muscle tension ☑
B   Decrease in perspiration ☐
C   Increase in pupil size ☑
D   Increase in salivation ☐   [2 marks]

You'd get two marks for this question — one mark for each correct answer.

In Some Questions You Might Need to Complete or Label a Diagram

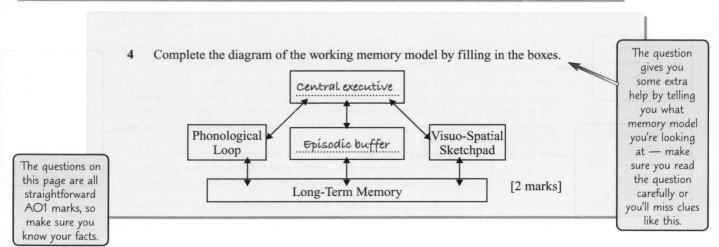

4   Complete the diagram of the working memory model by filling in the boxes.

Central executive

Phonological Loop   Episodic buffer   Visuo-Spatial Sketchpad

Long-Term Memory   [2 marks]

The question gives you some extra help by telling you what memory model you're looking at — make sure you read the question carefully or you'll miss clues like this.

The questions on this page are all straightforward AO1 marks, so make sure you know your facts.

Worked Exam

*You'll be Given Questions Where You Have to **Apply** Your **Knowledge***

For example, you could be given a **scenario**, and be asked to use your **knowledge** of psychology to explain it.

5   Read the item below and then answer the questions that follow.

> Roz is talking about her baby son, Charlie, to her friend.
> "It's wonderful how he knows I'm his mother. If he's crying, he always calms down as soon as I hold him. It's as if he knows I always feed him."

5.1 Give a brief definition of attachment.   [2 marks]

Attachment is a close emotional bond formed between two individuals. Attached infants show a desire to be close to their primary caregiver and will show distress when separated.

This is a good, full answer that would get both of the marks.

5.2 Explain how learning theory can be used to explain attachment.
Refer to Charlie and Roz in your answer.   [6 marks]

Learning theory uses conditioning to explain attachment. In classical conditioning, Charlie would learn associations between things in his environment. For example, being fed gives Charlie pleasure and his desire for food is fulfilled when Roz is there. In this way, an association is formed between Roz and Charlie's food. When Roz is close, Charlie will feel pleasure, so he'll desire to be close to her and form an attachment.

In operant conditioning, Charlie's behaviour is reinforced. Charlie will feel discomfort when he is hungry. He may discover that if he cries, his mother, Roz, will come and provide food, removing the discomfort. This is negative reinforcement. Roz becomes associated with food and Charlie will desire to be close to her, again showing attachment.

Use clear explanations of the two types of conditioning.

It's no good just explaining what learning theory is — you won't get very many marks. You need to talk about learning, associations and reinforcers in relation to Charlie and Roz.

Use psychological terms, e.g. 'conditioning' and 'reinforcement', where possible.

You might have to apply your knowledge to a scientific **study** or **procedure**.

6   Read the item below and then answer the question that follows.

> A psychologist wanted to investigate obedience levels. She set up an experiment where participants were asked to complete a mindless task which involved writing out the numbers 1-100, then ripping up the paper and starting again. She found that when instructions were given by a fellow participant, obedience levels were a lot lower than when they were given by a psychologist who was dressed in a white coat.

Outline how legitimacy of authority can influence obedience levels and explain how it has been illustrated in the procedure above.   [4 marks]

We are socialised to recognise figures of authority, such as police officers, parents, teachers, etc. They are legitimate authorities. This means we are more likely to obey them because they have a social role, in which they are respected.

In the procedure, the person giving the instructions was seen as a more legitimate authority figure when they were a psychologist dressed in a white coat, compared to a fellow participant. As a result, people were possibly more likely to trust the instructions from the psychologist as they believed that the psychologist had more knowledge than a participant.

Outline legitimate authorities first. Then you can go on to apply your knowledge.

You'll get two marks for outlining and two marks for explaining and applying your knowledge.

Worked Exam

Remember, **Research Method** Questions Could Appear **Anywhere...**

7 Read the item below, then answer the questions that follow.

> A memory study involved three groups of 6 participants:
>
> **Group A** repeated the word 'the' whilst learning a list of 15 words.
> **Group B** were asked to draw shapes whilst learning the same list.
> **Group C** acted as a control group and learnt the list with no distraction.
>
> The total numbers of words recalled are shown in the table below.
>
> | | Group A | Group B | Group C |
> |---|---|---|---|
> | **Total number of words recalled** | 48 | 72 | 80 |

> *When you're given a results table make sure you understand what it is showing. In this case it's the total number of words recalled by all of the participants in each group.*

7.1 State the type of design used in the experiment. **[1 mark]**

The experiment used an independent measures design.

> *Take a look at page 80 to remind yourself about the different experimental designs used in psychology.*

7.2 Give **one** disadvantage of using this experimental design. **[1 mark]**

Independent measures designs need more participants than repeated measures designs.

> *Independent measures designs can also be affected by participant variables.*

7.3 Write a hypothesis for this experiment. **[3 marks]**

There will be a difference in the number of words recalled when participants are asked to repeat a word, draw shapes, or have no distraction whilst learning a list of words.

> *Because the question doesn't specify, you can choose to write either a directional or non-directional hypothesis, or a null or alternative hypothesis.*

7.4 Explain why using a control group improved the experimental design of this study. **[2 marks]**

Participants in the control group performed the task with no distraction. Their performance could be used as a baseline. The performances of the experimental groups could then be compared to the control group to see the effect of the independent variable on the dependent variable.

> *This question would give you AO3 marks because you're being asked to analyse the research design.*

7.5 Calculate the mean number of words recalled by participants in Group A. Show your working. **[2 marks]**

Mean = total number of words recalled ÷ number of participants
*   = 48 ÷ 6 = 8 words*
So the mean number of words recalled by participants in Group A was 8.

> *You could be given the raw data and asked to work out the mean, median or mode directly.*

7.6 Calculate the total number of words recalled by Group A as a percentage of the total number of words recalled by the control group. **[2 marks]**

Group C total = 80. Group A total = 48.
(48 ÷ 80) × 100 = 60%
So Group A recalled 60% of the words recalled by the control group.

> *You could get a question asking you to draw a graph from some given data. Look at pages 99-103 to remind yourself of all the different types of graphs.*

Keep an Eye on the **Time**

- Time management is one of the most important exam skills to have.

- How **long** you spend on each question is really important in an exam — it could make all the difference to your grade.

- It doesn't matter if you **leave** some questions out to begin with.

- For example, if you're stuck on a question that's worth only a **few marks**, don't spend ages trying to answer it — you can always come back to it if you have time.

Tasha really wanted to answer her exam but it hadn't started ringing yet.

Worked Exam

You'll be Given Some **Extended Writing** Questions Too...

Take a look at this **outline** and **evaluate** question...

8   Outline and evaluate the working memory model.   [12 marks]

> For outline and evaluate questions, you'll get a mix of AO1 and AO3 marks.

> It's a good idea to start by saying why the model was developed in the first place.

The working memory model was developed by Baddeley and Hitch and expanded on the idea of the short-term store. They believed that rather than being one single store, the short-term store is an active processor which consists of several separate stores. The central executive oversees everything and can be described as 'attention'. It has a limited capacity and controls all of the other 'slave' systems.

> Before you start writing, it might help to draw a quick sketch of the model so you remember all the parts.

These other systems include the phonological loop, the visuo-spatial sketchpad and the episodic buffer (which was added to the model at a later date). The phonological loop holds speech-based information, and contains a phonological store (the inner ear) and an articulatory process (the inner voice). The visuo-spatial sketchpad temporarily holds visual and spatial information. Finally, the episodic buffer briefly stores information from other subsystems, and integrates it together, along with information gathered from the long-term memory. This allows everything to make sense.

The working memory model has a lot of support from other studies. One study by Gathercole and Baddeley illustrated the use of the visuo-spatial sketchpad. They split participants into two groups. Both groups had to follow a moving spot of light (visuo-spatial), but one group followed the spot whilst describing the angles on a letter (also visuo-spatial), whilst the other group had to do a verbal task (articulatory). Gathercole and Baddeley found that performance was much better when participants used different systems.

> Referencing other studies shows that you have a broad knowledge of the subject.

Shallice and Warrington also found support for the working memory model through a case study. Patient KF was brain-damaged and suffered with some STM loss. He was subsequently okay with visual tasks, but not with verbal tasks, and so it was concluded that he must have an intact visuo-spatial sketchpad, but an impaired articulatory loop.

> Don't forget to criticise the model too. No theory is ever perfect.

The model emphasises the fact that rehearsal is just one process that transfers information into the long-term memory, but it might not be the only method. This applies to real-life situations where memories do go straight to the long-term memory without rehearsal.

However, the model has been heavily criticised. It is seen to be too simplistic and vague. It doesn't explain how information is transferred to the long-term memory, and lots of the research into the model lacks ecological validity as it used laboratory studies.

> You can mention ecological validity when evaluating pretty much any psychological study. It either has it or it doesn't.

1) You'll have gathered that to write a good answer, you need to show **detailed** and **accurate** knowledge.

2) Basically, you need to show the examiner that you **understand** stuff really well.

3) Picking out studies and theories to **support** your answers is great — but keep it all **relevant** to the question.

Make a **Plan** Before You Start Your Answer

- The **quality** of your writing will also be assessed — so make sure you use **good English** with **specialist psychology vocabulary** where appropriate.

- Try to **structure** your answer in an **organised** way. Your answer needs to be **clear** and **coherent**. Before you start, it's worth jotting down a quick **plan** of what you want to write so that you don't just end up with a really jumbled answer full of **irrelevant information**.

For example, if a question asks you to discuss a psychological model with reference to a theoretical or practical context, your plan might look something like this:

1. Brief description of the model
2. Apply the model to the context
3. Evaluate the model

DO WELL IN YOUR EXAMS

Index

Index

Index

Index

Index